How To
DOUBLE
YOUR WEDDING BUSINESS
IN 12 MONTHS

Britaeyi

FAB Them To Death!

CHRIS EVANS
North America's Foremost
Wedding Business Expert

Forward by Bill Heaton

Double Profit - All in one year!

It appears that there will be a "big spike" in wedding related business sales if everyone reads and puts into practice the principles and points contained within this fabulous book. As an entrepreneur and lawyer for over thirty years, I have seen it all, until Chris Evans' book came along.

Evans deserves congratulations for writing *How to Double Your Wedding Business in 12 Months*, a book that focuses on the number one goal for every wedding-related business owner: profit. It is profit that helps businesses grow and allows us to provide better and better products and services to brides and grooms on the most important day of their lives.

By focusing on profit, Evans offers up a clear and concise roadmap to wedding business bliss, providing a solid analysis of the marketing and promotional options available to wedding businesses, along with a well thought-out guide to generating successful returns for your hard-earned media dollars.

And with all the media clutter in the world today, numerous wedding magazines, a plethora of bridal shows, and more wedding planning websites than you can shake a stick at, that's an important thing to know.

They say without advertising that nothing happens. But if you make uninformed choices in advertising your wedding business, even worse can happen, especially in this economy, where any decision can make or break your business.

Through this book, Evans has removed the smoke and mirrors from media and promotional decisions in an easy-to-read, realistic format, based on his actual years of experience in working with wedding-related businesses that are seeking to sell their products or services to the bridal consumer. It's a practical, step-by-step guide to the age-old dilemma of choosing media that will convert to more wedding-related sales—in the quickest possible time—perhaps even lightening speed.

Ultimately, in today's economy, generating real sales from your media investment is vital to the success of your business. You need more bang for your buck than ever before, and Evans tells you just how to get it.

He doesn't just offer up theories; his book is a practical, down to earth, easy to understand "seminar" for those looking for wedding business success. His fundamental lessons in getting appointments, making presentations, and selling to the bride and groom are invaluable to everyone in the wedding business, regardless of whether you are a years-long veteran or a new business just starting out. This is the tried-and–true stuff that works.

So, read the *How to Double Your Wedding Business in 12 Months* and don't sweat the small stuff. Implement what Evans says, and you'll be on your way to complete bliss and **profit in the wedding industry**.

Bill Heaton
President/CEO
The Great Bridal Expo Group, Inc.
Bridal Expo, Inc.

Notes from Other Wedding Professionals

"I have been a Bridal Show Producer for 25 years. I am currently the Director of the Bridal Shows Producers International and owner of Bridesclub.com. I have not only watched Chris teach his sales methods to hundreds of wedding merchants, I have actually taught Chris's sales techniques to hundreds of my own wedding merchants. The Evans Sales Solutions, Inc. 'sales methods' has helped the wedding industry achieve financial prosperity. It just simply works.

"I have found the principles he teaches take your company to the next level. It gives wedding professionals 'the very point-by-point method' they need to succeed. If more wedding merchants would use Chris's system in sales, they would be 'Doubling Their Business EVERY YEAR'!"

Brad Buckles
Wedding Expos/ Hawaii Bridal Expos, Owner & Operator
Director of Bridal Show Producers International, 2008-2010

"Chris's seminars, book, and training represent the best value in training I have ever received. His book is chock full of useful and vital information and 'wedding industry trade secrets'. I was able to double my DJ business in only a few short months, allowing me to branch out to photography and video using Chris's techniques."

Darryl Bryant
Totally Entertainment

"This is simply the best training I have ever received for my business. I truly believe the ideas and techniques Chris shares in this book will be of value for all businesses, not just wedding businesses. It was as if Chris knew the problems I have had with my advertising and he wrote the book to address my needs. This is a must read for every wedding business."

Jamison Taylor
Taylor'd Memories Event Planning & Decor

"I wish I had read this book fifteen years ago!"

Kevin Lister
Pasadena Flowers

> *"[I]t appears that there will be a "big spike" in wedding related business sales if everyone reads and puts into practice the principles and points contained within this fabulous book. As an entrepreneur and lawyer for over thirty years, I have seen it all, until Chris Evans' book came along." - Bill Heaton, President/CEO, The Great Bridal Expo Group, Inc.*

How To
DOUBLE
YOUR WEDDING BUSINESS
IN 12 MONTHS

THE ROADMAP TO
SUCCESS FOR
WEDDING PROFESSIONALS

CHRIS EVANS

NORTH AMERICA'S FOREMOST
WEDDING BUSINESS EXPERT

Thank you to my wife, Rebekah, and my family, Jamison, Chris II, and Sagan. I appreciate your unconditional support in everything I do.

Thank you to Debi Ryono for all the hard work editing this book, as well as the love and friendship.

A special thank you to Tom Hopkins, who I believe is the finest sales trainer on the planet. The systems and techniques Tom taught me over the years have allowed me to take a small, home-based business and build it beyond what I thought possible and far more than I deserve.

Tom's dedication to helping salespeople become more professional has enriched the lives of thousands, and I am one of the fortunate people who learned (and continue to learn) from his lessons. Inevitably, Tom will be reflected through my sales process. I hope I make him proud.

Contents

Maximize Your Results from This Book

This book is written to show you how to double the size of your wedding business and get more out of life. Obviously, though, the secret to success is to do more than just read. I encourage you to use a highlighter to mark sections you believe are important or invest in the companion *How to Double Your Wedding Business in 12 Months Workbook*. Anything you can do to make this book a more effective tool will help you grow your business and double your sales!

It's important as you study the techniques highlighted in this book that you memorize and implement them in your daily business. There isn't much benefit from simply reading about a great way to grow your business, but not taking action.

Web Support

To assist you in your growth I want to encourage you to visit www.EvansSalesSolutions.com. We have crafted the website to provide you with a wide range of services and support as you move towards growing your business. Evans Sales Solutions, Inc. offers everything from free downloads of informative and motivating articles to one-on-one coaching opportunities, crafted for your specific business.

Our primary goal when we created Evans Sales Solutions, Inc. was to help you succeed. As a wedding professional, I know how frustrating and challenging it can be to have less business and higher costs than you want. Most wedding professionals entered the business because it was fun, but somewhere along the line, it became hard work. We want to lighten your load, and while it may always be work, we're going to make it work you can love more than ever. You're going to make a small investment of money and time. You may even select business or personal coaching to help you along the way, but I can promise you this, we will do everything we can to help you achieve the goals you set.

Thank you

CHAPTER 1 – It Begins

My first experience with selling laid the groundwork for my future by teaching me the basic principles I would need to know about selling. I didn't fully realize at the time that what I was learning would be instrumental in my day-to-day life, but I did soon realize something important had happened.

Like most kids who grew up in the 60's, I enjoyed reading comic books. But, unlike most kids in the 60's, I enjoyed reading the advertisements in the back of the comic books (I still look at the small ads in the back of most magazines) as much as the comics themselves. My adventure into sales began when I picked up a copy of the latest comic book and noticed an advertisement promising I could earn hundreds of dollars by selling seeds door-to-door.

I read and reread the ad. It told me that all I needed to do was order their ready-made sales kit. The kit came complete with instructions and a success guide as well as my first set of seeds. Once I received the kit, I would be well on my way to fame and fortune with door-to-door selling.

I remember my hands shaking as I filled in the form for my Sales Success Kit. I was totally excited about the possibility of making money and earning cool prizes like the x-ray vision glasses! I talked my grandmother out of a 10-cent stamp and ran to the mailbox to send off my order. As a 12-year-old does, I started checking the mailbox every day, waiting for my kit to arrive. It never occurred to me it might take a week or two for the company to process my order. In my mind, I'd mailed them the order, and it was time for them to send me my kit. I wanted to get started!

It went on like this for at least two months. With each passing day, I became more and more discouraged. What success could I have with a company that couldn't find the time to deliver the product to me? Then I noticed a similar ad for a different company in another comic book. Company number two offered to provide the seeds, a training manual, and a complete success guide, just like the first company, but as an added bonus, if I were one of the first fifty people to return the order form, I would receive a unique box with a handle that would allow me to carry my seeds door-to-door. Once again filled with hope, I filled in the order form, found a 10-cent stamp, dropped the registration form in the mailbox, and waited for my seeds to arrive.

Company number two obviously had a much better system of delivering their product than company number one. My seeds arrived in a little over one week, and I was thrilled as I dug into the box to see what was inside. I was a little surprised the training manual wasn't much more than a sheet of paper, and the success guide was smaller than the comic books where I saw the ad in the first place, but I was undeterred. I reviewed the information, practiced the script, and decided I would start the next day, making my fortune by selling seeds door-to-door. I ripped out the last page of the training manual, filled in my name, and asked my mother to sign the certificate proving I had completed the training program. I carried the certificate with me at every sales presentation.

It really wasn't hard for a 12-year-old to sell seeds door-to-door in the 1960's. Most of the safety concerns we have today about kids going door-to-door were certainly not as prevalent back then. My mother had some concerns, but she agreed to allow me to strike out and make my fortune as long as I did it within the confines of our neighborhood. Even at 12, I realized my mother was forcing me into an undesirable situation by limiting my market potential, but I figured once I had sold to everyone in my neighborhood, she would have to let me expand my territory. Frankly, I knew I would cross that bridge when I came to it.

A sales presentation went something like this:

> "Hello, my name is Chris, and I work for the World's Best Seed Company! I'm trying to earn a trip to Disneyland, or any one of a bunch of valuable prizes, and I'd like to know if you would like to enhance the beauty of your home with flowers. The World's Best Seed Company has provided me with a full

selection of seeds, and I'd like to give you an opportunity to select them from the kit I have right here."

I would hold the seed box up in front of them, and more often than not, they would buy a few packets. If they seemed reluctant or they couldn't find any seeds they liked, I would throw in some incentive. I would mention a unique opportunity, good for today and today only. They could purchase one package of seeds for one dollar, or three packages of seeds for two dollars. I only used the "special offer" when it appeared somebody was being reluctant about buying my seeds. After all, I was on a mission.

It must have worked, because I sold a lot of seeds!

One of the experiences I had, while offering my seeds, provided my first big lesson in sales. Walking down the street and looking for another place to make a sale, a particular house caught my eye. I had walked by it many times before, but I did not know who lived there. As I approached the door, I saw flowers and decorations on the front of the house, and I knew that translated into a high probability that this person would buy my seeds. I pictured knocking on the door and having some nice little old lady answer it. I knew I was going to have a pleasant conversation. Primed and ready to sell, I rang the doorbell.

Given what I expected, imagine my shock when the door swung open and a very rotund man stood there looking at me. He had a stubbly beard and a t-shirt that stopped about three inches above his hairy navel. He had a cigarette hanging out of his mouth and towered over me by a good three feet. He was scowling and looked like he was about to hit me at any moment.

This man's presence completely threw me off my normal presentation. Instead of mentioning that I worked for the World's Best Seed Company and letting him know I was trying to earn money and work toward a trip to Disneyland, I stumbled out something like, "I've got some seeds here. You don't want to buy any, do you?"

I was even more shocked when he looked at the box and said, "What type of seeds do you have?" Unable to think of what to say, I simply held the box up and let him pick through the seeds. He hadn't given me an objection, but as if disembodied, I heard my voice saying, "You can buy one pack for a dollar or three packs for two dollars." I was in shock; somebody used my voice and gave him the special offer. I had given him a DISCOUNT, and he hadn't said a word! It took me a second to realize those words had come from my mouth. My mind may have been confused, but my body knew what to do. It had obviously slipped into survival mode and figured the only way out of this alive was to offer a discount. At that moment, I was cheering my body on! I just wanted to live.

He simply grunted and continued digging into my box of seeds. After what seemed like an eternity (30 seconds in real-world time, tops), he pulled out four packs of seeds and handed me a $10 bill. "Keep the change," he said. I was speechless. Before I could stutter out a "thank you", he simply closed the door.

In a matter of a few seconds, I had gone from sheer terror to the sweet smell of victory! I took a deep breath and felt the fresh air enter my body and fill it with the nectar of life and as H2O seeped into my being. I felt an electrical impulse start at the top of my head and rush to my feet. I was locked in place, not wanting to move, as I celebrated the fact that I had both lived and made the most profitable sale of my career. It took me a few moments to compose myself.

As I walked away from his house, it occurred to me: I did everything wrong, yet I still managed to get the sale! I really didn't do anything to earn the sale, other than knock on the door, but in this particular case, it was enough. The simple fact I had taken it upon myself to go out on a hot Las Vegas afternoon and knock on doors meant I had made more money in one sale than my buddy Rory made in an entire week on his paper route, and I got to sleep-in during the summer. Life was good.

I'm glad to say, I still get the same wild exhilaration today when my company makes a sale.

What important things did I learn from this experience?

1) You can never judge a prospect by their looks. When this man answered the door, he was the last person I expected would buy seeds from me. I thought I had a much better chance of being beaten up than I did at selling anything. It was only because I was scared to death and my legs were locked that I even stood there and did somewhat of a presentation. I had judged him strictly on appearance. Had I not worked through my fear and stood there while he looked at my seeds, I would have never made the sale.

2) Even when the presentation is going in a direction other than what is expected, it is still very possible to close the sale. In fact, rarely will a presentation go as planned. As professional salespeople, we need to be prepared for as many different scenarios as possible.

3) You need a track to run on. You need to be prepared with a basic organized presentation that you have memorized. Consider it your "fall-back plan"—having it ready allows you to fall back on instinct when you lose track of everything else.

4) Never put your face near a large man's navel. It truly is a scary thing.

There was another lesson I learned through the experience of selling seeds door-to-door. About two weeks later, after I had sold three full boxes of seeds from World's Best Seed Company, I received a box of seeds from the first company I had requested seeds from. It was the original order I had placed and given up on. My mother took me to the post office and helped me return the box to the company unopened. I've had a few people ask why I didn't just sell that company's seeds as well, and maybe I should have. However, even at 12, I felt there should be some loyalty to the company that responded and did things right. I even had the training sheet that named me an Official Representative, because I completed the training program.

What's the point? Company number one completely blew it. It had an enthusiastic, motivated, very willing salesperson that would have sold a lot of seeds for it, yet its system was so slow that it lost the opportunity to derive income from my work. Even at 12 years old, I knew company number one had to make some major changes, or it was going to go out of business.

My Advertising Isn't Working – Why?

If you are a wedding professional, chances are, you have invested some of your hard-earned money in advertising, hoping to expand your business and increase your market.

As a fellow businessperson in the wedding industry, I know it's rare not to be contacted at least once a week by some new wedding magazine, bridal show, wedding web page, newspaper, television station, radio station, or advertising outlet, all claiming to have the perfect way for you to generate business.

Chances are also very good that after you invested your money, you were thrilled to see your advertising in print or hear your message on the radio. Maybe the booth you designed for the bridal show was so perfect; it brought a tear to your eye. Maybe the television commercial made you proud as you watched it play on the local cable station. It's fun to see your message reaching out to the masses, and obviously, advertising is a very big business. You only have to open a newspaper, flip through a magazine, or listen to the radio to find advertising messages from hundreds of businesses.

It's also very likely that after the advertising ran, you struggled to determine if it was worth the investment. Did you truly get any additional sales that you wouldn't have received without the advertisement? Did you make more money than you spent? Why didn't the radio campaign make your phone ring off the hook? Why didn't the huge newspaper ad generate thousands of calls? In fact, why didn't the advertising generate any calls at all?

What about the bridal show where you had such a great booth? Hundreds of brides stopped and talked with you. You gave out hundreds of fliers, and you were dead tired on Sunday night. Why haven't you received hundreds of telephone calls, emails, and walk-ins, all eager to book your service? Why is your show success dependent upon chasing down the brides from a mailing list provided after the show? Do you really have to invest hundreds of dollars more in direct mail and telephone calls—not to mention your own time—just to see a profit?

There's a very logical reason why you may not do as well in your advertising as you think you should. There are identifiable causes and actions that limit your success and cause your advertising to fail. In fact, few in wedding advertising will admit one underlying truth. I hesitate to call it a "dirty little secret", because that implies some conspiracy or deception, and it's not. It's simply a truth:

The majority of advertising sold to wedding professionals does not work unless you know the secret to successful advertising!

It doesn't matter if it's a wedding magazine, newspaper, bridal insert, bridal show, radio, direct mail, web page, or television commercial, they simply do not work all the time. You invest in your advertising with high hopes and great dreams about the huge amount of business you will receive. Unfortunately, reality rarely meets expectation. For the most part, you're lucky to break even and recoup the cost of the program.

It's an interesting problem and possibly the main reason you purchased this book. The companies producing the advertising are not intentionally misleading you or delivering a faulty product. In fact, I believe there are many great opportunities for you to invest in advertising and to make it work extremely well. It's simply a case in which the average wedding professional doesn't have the time, money, or expertise to make advertising work for them, and most wedding professionals are so focused on their business that they don't implement simple steps that will make their advertising a success!

Let's use the wedding magazine as an example:

Bridal magazines reach thousands of brides. Statistics show more than 80 percent of brides purchase a wedding magazine, and thousands more pick up copies of the free wedding magazine/planners typically found in bridal salons. If you have worked in the wedding business for any length of time, you will know it's an indisputable fact: *Brides love to look at wedding magazines.*

If a wedding magazine distributes thousands of copies in your market and the vast majority of brides love to look at bridal magazines, doesn't it make sense that you should have an advertisement in the magazine?

On the surface, it appears simple. Buying advertising in the magazine should generate a significant number of incoming telephone calls and bridal visits that you can convert into sales. It may appear simple, but it's not.

I've met thousands of wedding professionals who have purchased beautiful, well-placed ads in many different bridal magazines. In most cases, the magazines are delivered exactly as promised, yet the wedding professional will tell you that it was not a wise investment. The advertisement reaped little or no reward. In most cases, the sales made from the ad didn't cover the cost to run it.

How is it possible that a very successful magazine, one the brides love to read, may generate only a handful of phone calls? As an advertiser, this wouldn't be a problem if the magazine allowed you to pay based on response, but to the best of my knowledge, wedding magazines want thousands of dollars for the advertising with no guarantee of success.

Throughout this book, we are going to analyze the various advertising opportunities available to your business. We will take an in-depth, no-holds-barred look at the realities and myths about each. We will explore why advertising fails and how you can ensure that you never have an unprofitable advertising campaign again.

We will expose the truth of why your advertising doesn't work and show you a proven program that will allow you to double your wedding business in the next 12 months.

My Story – Part 1

The easiest way to begin our journey together is to provide some background information so that you can understand where I've been and what I've done to have the experiences I've had. After all, my experiences in the wedding business and the things I've learned along the way are what I'm going to be sharing with you in this book. In effect, my experiences and the systems I've developed from them are going to dictate whether you truly can double your wedding business in the next 12 months.

Frankly, I had no intention of being involved in the wedding business for the long-term. Like many of you, I found myself working within the wedding industry because of an ongoing chain of supposedly unrelated events that led me to the point where, one day, I woke up and found myself a bridal show producer with more than 200 shows to my credit.

My journey into the wedding business actually began back in the 1970s when I was looking for part-time work during high school. Growing up in Las Vegas, Nevada, presented many opportunities for employment within the hotel and convention industry. I was lucky to secure a job with Las Vegas Convention Service, a major coordinator of trade shows in the city. I started out by running various supplies from one location to another for the show managers. I would arrive at the main office each morning, find out what particular trade show I was working that day, and then go to the convention center to do whatever had to be done to ensure a successful event. It was interesting to work in a very adult, and somewhat tainted, industry in Las Vegas as a high school student. It quickly became apparent the exhibitors at many of the conventions cared less about business than about having a three-day party in Las Vegas.

Over a period of time, and as I became older, my job responsibilities changed from being a "gopher" to a "convention coordinator" and having the ability to work on some of the larger conventions. It was a perfect job at that time. Eventually, I took classes at the University of Nevada, Las Vegas, while maintaining my employment with Las Vegas Convention Service. Conventions tend to require you to work odd hours, and for a college student, the sporadic nature of the work was perfect. Not to mention, the money was great.

After a shot at college, I worked in the retail business, was married, and, ultimately, ended up in Fresno, California, as manager of an Aaron Brothers Art Mart. I could write another book about the things I learned at Aaron Brothers. They were unique characters and truly great businessmen. After arriving in Fresno, I realized the retail business did not offer the long-term opportunity or income I needed, and I quickly moved on to other opportunities.

Prior to my first daughter being born, I had a bright idea. This was in 1980 before everybody on the planet had a video camera in their phone. Video cameras were new, and people would stare at them, wondering how they worked. It occurred to me that if you owned a video camera, and you were to contact a bride-to-be, she might be interested in having her wedding videotaped. I started talking to my wife about buying a video camera, which, at the time, was about a $3,000 investment with an additional $1,800 for the bulky video recorder you had to carry over your shoulder. I wasn't concerned about the fact that we didn't have $5,000 to buy the system; I just knew that if I got my hands on a video camera, I could find a way to make money. Additionally, I'd have a camera to videotape of my daughter. After badgering my wife for several weeks, she finally relented and agreed we could take a loan to buy the video equipment.

The next problem we faced was finding the video equipment. At that time, there wasn't any place in Fresno where you could purchase it. We had to drive 250 miles to Los Angeles and visit two or three major electronics stores before we found one that actually had the new video equipment in stock. Even the salesman who was demonstrating the equipment for us was in awe of the camera. I remember, he had to check with his boss, because he wasn't sure the camera recorded sound and video. He thought that it only captured the video without the sound! I bought the camera, recorder, tripod, and 10 videotapes (which at the time were $22.50 each), loaded it in the car, and headed back to Fresno. We had $5,800 invested in video equipment and not a clue if my idea to shoot weddings would work.

While I continued to work my day job, I started looking in the daily legal paper to see who had secured marriage licenses. The Internet didn't exist yet, so I used a reverse directory or telephone book for phone numbers so that I could call the bride-to-be.

The calls would go something like this:

"Hello! This is Chris with Video Pro. I understand you're getting married next week, and I was calling to see if you had anyone who was videotaping your wedding?"

At which point the bride-to-be would usually say something like, "You want to do what at my wedding?"

The videotaping of weddings, at the time, was just unheard of. Brides routinely said things like, "We don't have a videotape player," or, "We're not interested."

It wasn't long before I realized that calling people from a legal paper didn't provide enough lead-time before the weddings. People pulled their marriage license just a day or two before their wedding, and I was reaching them too late. I started to look around for a way to reach the bride-to-be earlier in the process. I thought it was logical to contact the bridal shops and tux shops to see if there might be a way I could get leads from them.

At this point, I heard about something called a bridal show. Compared to today's bridal expos, it was small. In Fresno, there were about 40 exhibitors who were all members of a local bridal association; as a member of the association, you could participate in their annual bridal show. The association was run by a tux-shop owner, and it was limited to three of any one type of business— three bridal shops, three tux shops, three flower shops, etc.—and they did not even have a category for videography.

I contacted the association president for an application and submitted it to the selection committee, which required a personal interview before being accepted into the group.

It was a happy day when I received the membership letter saying I had been accepted into the association. I immediately registered two other video companies, because I saw the potential of being the only video provider in the association. Frankly, I think the only reason they let me get away with doing that was nobody seemed to believe the videotaping of weddings was going to be that big. At the time, the quality of video and the amount of money it took to become involved in the wedding video industry were two major reasons most professional photographers laughed when it came to videography. To a certain extent, they projected an air of superiority, which didn't disappear until the videographers started cutting into the profit margins of the photographers. It was then that many photographers decided that wedding videos were an interesting sideline that, of course, became necessary for every wedding. It's interesting how the profit motive is such a great stimulator of attitudes.

Having had a background in trade shows, I started to plan for my bridal-show experience, like I have planned for a trade show in Las Vegas. We designed a backdrop with built-in TV screens, and we had a platform in the middle of the display wall where brides could step up and have an engagement portrait taken. Once the bride registered with us, we promised to deliver her engagement portrait within a week or two after the event. At the time, e-mail didn't exist, so we had to physically deliver each portrait to every bride-to-be. It was a wonderful way to schedule visits and have the time we needed to explain what we provided to the brides-to-be.

During our second year in business, Video Pro videotaped more than 300 weddings. At one point, we had the vast majority of students from the Fresno State Audio/Video department working for us. Quite an amazing feat, given that we had to explain to each and every bride-to-be what our product was before we could convince her to allocate a portion of her wedding budget to us.

During this time, it became obvious to me that the bridal shows were good, but with a little bit of work, they could be great. It was interesting that while all the members of the association contributed equally to produce the show, the bridal shops and the tux shops received an inordinate amount of exposure to the brides. Those shops stopped the entire event for one or two hours a day to present their products in a fashion show, which, in effect, was a one-on-one commercial for their products, while I stood off in the corner wondering when I would have an opportunity to talk to the brides again. I know that women at a bridal expos love the fashion shows, but it occurred to me that there had to be a better way.

As with most things in life, many challenges present many opportunities, and that's exactly what happened.

To be continued...

CHAPTER 2 – Where Am I?

To start on the road to doubling your wedding business in the next 12 months, I would like you to do a very simple exercise. On the next page, you'll see the outline of a heart. I think it's appropriate, being in the wedding business, that we should use a heart.

What I'd like you to do is take a moment and think about what it would take to double your wedding business in the next year. Now, I'm not talking about the process or the system you have to go through to double your wedding business. We're going to show you that further on. What I want you to think about is what doubling your wedding business looks like. In other words, how many weddings would it take you to double your wedding business?

If you're a photographer and worked 50 weddings last year, it's very simple: You need a hundred weddings this year to double your wedding business.

If you'd rather think about it in terms of dollars earned, you can do it that way too. You may prefer to say; "We did $50,000 in business this year, so this next year we wanted $100,000." However, ultimately, you must convert that number into how many weddings it represents.

Take a moment now and write in the middle of that heart how many weddings it would take to double your business.

Now that you've identified the number that represents doubling your wedding business, I'd like to talk to you about the five essential steps to increasing your sales.

Every business should have a business plan that it follows. It's been my experience because many wedding professionals came into the business almost by accident; they don't have a business plan. Very often, I meet people who started working with brides, almost as a hobby, and then their business grows to a point where it can support them. Many enjoyed working on their own wedding so much that they made the decision to become full-time wedding professionals.

It's a fact that the vast majority of wedding-related businesses in the United States are still mom-and-pop organizations. Just a few short years ago, there was no such thing as a national chain of bridal stores. Every market had a collection of independent shops that set the standard for bridal-gown sales in each community. It's common in these smaller businesses that no plan exists for growth or advertising. You might say that most of the businesses that deal with the brides use the trial-and-error method of business planning and advertising.

In order to eliminate some of the errors, we're going to take a look at five essential steps to increase your sales.

The steps are as follows:

- Establish your current position.
- Develop a sales plan.
- Implement the plan.
- Measure for success and adjust.
- Go back to number one.

Let's look at each of the steps in order.

Establish Your Current Position
You need to know where you are before you can measure the success and move forward toward growth. After all, if you're not

aware of what your current position is, there's no way you can measure the success or failure of any advertising you do. In a very limited sense, that's what the heart exercise was about. We want to establish, in a quick and easy manner, some number that you can shoot for so you can measure your progress as you move toward doubling your business.

Clearly, we didn't look at in-depth market analysis. We didn't decide on profit margin, and we certainly didn't look at competition and the effects of supply and demand on your business. These are all elements that must be considered in an overall business plan, but are beyond the scope of this book. We are going to concentrate on my hands-on processes you must go through to double your wedding business. I'm confident that once your sales start to take off, you will have both the financial resources and the time to develop a full business and marketing plan.

For now, we're going to concentrate on what it would take to double your business in the next 12 months. Having completed the heart exercise, you now have a specific number that you can shoot for over the next 12 months. If you reach that number, you will know that you've come very close to doubling your wedding business. You also know what you need on a monthly, and even weekly, basis if you are going to double your business. At this point, please divide your goal by 48 (you're going to take four weeks off), and we have your weekly sales goal.

To truly establish your current position, you will need to perform a much more detailed analysis of your business. Nevertheless, for our purposes, the general number you wrote down will work.

Develop a Sales Plan

I understand that most wedding professionals don't have total control of their day-to-day activities, so it may be slightly unrealistic to think that they would have a written sales plan in place. While it's true that a written sales plan could help your business, it's also true that the vast majority of business owners are so busy taking care of the day-to-day operations that they tend to rely on experience and instincts as opposed to creating a written plan. One of the things we hope to do with this book—and if you have it, the companion workbook—is to help you create a sales plan to guide your business.

Having said that, I'd like to encourage you make sure to get not just a professionally written business plan, but also to make sure that an integral part of the plan is a sales plan. Once you're done reading this book, you will be far more qualified than most of your competitors to create a comprehensive sales plan. You will have a significant advantage in all forms of advertising and marketing because of the time you've taken to read this book. Now, it's important for you to take what you've learned and commit to a written sales plan to benefit your business.

At this point, I want to let you in on a secret. I know of a way for you to have a professionally produced business plan, written by an MBA, for hundreds, rather than thousands of dollars. I've done it, and the plans are wonderfully crafted, easily implemented, and are as professional as anything a major corporation can create. How do you do it?

Outsourcing

There are thousands of incredibly qualified business professionals throughout the world who are looking for work and can easily complete a comprehensive business or sales plan for you. This is one of the best-kept secrets of the Internet. You can hire a qualified professional to create a plan for you and reap significant savings. The lack of planning and the chaos it causes is one of the major reasons we formed Chris Evans International.

Now, wedding professionals can go to one place to find most of their business plan, marketing plan, and business consulting advice they need. EvansSalesSolutions.com specializes in wedding-industry businesses, and you will be sure to get the most comprehensive information geared toward your business.

Implement the Plan

Step number three in the process is to implement any plan that you create. While it seems like common sense, I've met many owners who created detailed plans and then allowed those plans to sit on a shelf, gathering dust. The great intentions the person had when the plan came back from the consultant were replaced by the tyranny of the urgent, and while everyone knew the plan existed, nobody actually took steps to implement it.

When you are done with this book, you will have a general idea about what your sales plan should be. It will be your choice whether to implement it or not. I can only hope that after taking the time to read this book and develop a plan, you won't let it languish on a shelf.

Occasionally, I'll be speaking with someone who's attended an educational seminar or some company training, and they will say something like: "I attended a seminar recently, and most of what I heard, I already knew. Then, I heard that one idea that made it all worthwhile. I'm glad I went."

Somewhere along the line, people have come to believe that they can read a book or attend a seminar, and if they get one useful idea, it's been worth it.

But, if I'm going to invest my time and money attending a seminar or reading a book, I want to get as many good ideas as possible. Before I invest $20 or $30 on the book or hundreds of dollars on a seminar, I want to know that I'm going to get tons of good ideas. That's what I have designed this book to deliver! I want you to learn many great techniques and ideas that you can implement on a daily basis to make your business a success. While I'm doing my best to give you great ideas, you have to do your part by committing to implement the sales plan when we are done.

I've seen hundreds of wedding professionals participate in advertising programs, where they generate a list after the program is over. Most bridal-show producers dutifully send a list of all the brides who attended the show within a week or two of the event. For the most part, exhibitors have come to expect these lists and some wedding professionals won't even consider participating in the show unless they receive a list of brides who attended.

Yet, I can think back on literally hundreds of wedding professionals I visited over the years who have the mailing list from prior shows sitting on the shelf, never opened. It's a classic case of great intentions, but poor implementation.

Implementation of the sales plan is crucial for success.

Measure Success and Adjust

This is so simple and obvious, yet many wedding professionals fail to do it. As you move through the process of increasing your sales, you need to compare what's actually happening each day against the sales plan and make adjustments. There will always be those areas that either exceed or fall short of your goals. It's important to track them religiously and make adjustments as required.

I want to caution you about taking time away from actually performing your business and wasting time managing your business. I've seen numerous wedding professionals get so wrapped up in managing the day-to-day operations that they don't have time to do whatever it is that they do. For example, I knew a photographer who would spend 50 or 60 hours a week at his computer managing his business, and of course, the more time he spent managing his business, the less time he spent shooting photographs. The fewer photographs he shot, the smaller his income became. He continued on this course of spending 10 times as much time managing his business as he spent performing his business, and it was only a few months before he had a major financial crisis on his hands. Fortunately, he was able to adjust his behavior and save his business before he passed the point of no return.

While it's important to measure your success and adjust as needed, it's also important to keep track of your time and make sure you are performing a function for which you get paid. If you're not careful, you can literally manage your business into failure. It's possible to be so organized and have so many programs in place that you can be a model in your industry, yet be a failure and out of business within a few months.

We want to find a happy medium, where we measure our success and adjust, without becoming so fixated on measuring that we hurt our business.

Go Back to Number One

This may be one of the most discouraging of the five essential steps to increasing your sales. I've seen many wedding-related businesses over the years become very successful after they participated in a radio commercial, a television commercial, or maybe the largest bridal show in the area. They were very successful, and they booked a lot of business. Then, over a period of time, they took their formula for success and made small changes.

There's an old saying that if it isn't broken, don't fix it. This is important for the wedding professional. I've seen wedding professionals book so many weddings from a bridal show that the next year, they've called the show promoter and said, "We can't handle all the business, so we're not going to participate in this year's show."

One year later, those same wedding professionals called the promoter to say, "Business is slow. Can we have our booth back?" It's shocking to me that they don't understand the reason that business is slow is because they stopped doing what was successful. They had a system that was working well and generating business, but instead of adjusting their business internally and expanding their sales, they chose to limit their success by eliminating the very source of their success.

They didn't have a plan to measure their success, and without a plan, you won't know what do when things are slow or when things are busy. In this case, when the time came for them to evaluate their position, they did go back to number one and started all over again. Business is a continuous cycle of peaks and valleys; it's important for you to have a plan to follow.

Our job in this book is to help you design the plan. Your job when you're done reading is to implement the plan.

CHAPTER 3: Keep Your Head in the Game

Over the years, I've met countless wedding professionals who started their business as a small mom-and-pop operation, many times as a hobby. Over time, the ventures grew to substantial size, and in the process, they made a good living. I find it interesting that one pattern repeats itself over and over again as these people become successful. I've noticed that most of them have a tendency to move away from what has worked successfully for them in the past, and they try new things, much of which doesn't work as well as what they been doing.

I understand that there's a tendency to get tired of doing the same thing over and over, but when it comes to business, you need to spend the majority of your time doing what you know is successful. Then spend a small portion of your time trying new things. Countless times, I've seen wedding professionals stop participating in successful advertising to try new or different advertising, as if they can only do one or the other.

It would be foolish to suggest the new marketing opportunities or new ideas should not be tried just because what you been doing in the past has been successful. On the other hand, it's equally as foolish to abandon proven programs of the past just because you're tired of doing them. I've found that most wedding professionals reach a comfort level that in the end is detrimental to their business.

I call it the "Success Factor". It seems like the more success entrepreneurs achieve, the more likely they are to abandon or change what has worked for them in the past because their success has gotten in the way. When you forget to do the basics that established your business just because you have reached a success plateau, you may find yourself slipping backwards, quickly forfeiting your success of the past. In short, their success led them to failure.

Balboa Island Success

I once had an opportunity to work with a disc jockey that ran a business from Balboa Island in Newport Beach, California. When I first met this young man, he was single, driving around in a beat-up old van, and had one, old, DJ system that he literally was holding together with masking tape. He had asked me to come explain a bridal-show opportunity we were offering. When I first met him, I didn't know if he had the ability to make an investment in marketing his businesses at a bridal show, but as the presentation progressed, it became obvious that he understood the importance of marketing his new business and was committed to investing the required funds to participate in the event. He reserved a booth and enrolled in one of our Merchant Maximizer Seminars, which were the predecessors of this book.

He attended the seminars, seemed to be taking consistent notes, and asked many questions. It was obvious that he was in his "sponge mode"—a time when we soak up everything around us no matter how insignificant it seems. He was an informational sponge.

At the show itself, I noticed that he was implementing many of the techniques we discussed in the seminar, and sure enough, it wasn't long before I heard from him again. He told me that the show had been a stellar success. Over the next few years, his business grew. It has always been my practice to have a post-event Merchant Appreciation Dinner. We invite all the show exhibitors to a great restaurant, serve them a fantastic meal, and encourage them to provide feedback on how the event went for them and what we can do better in the future. It's our way of saying thank you to the exhibitors whom we believe are the reason for the show. At most of the Merchant Appreciation Dinners, he would stand up and say how thankful he was for the seminars and for the show and how he believed it was because of our bridal shows and the fact that we held training seminars that he was becoming more and more successful.

Over a period of a few years, he was married, opened an office, and hired a substantial staff. He had many different types of sound systems that he could use at various weddings. His equipment became more professional as did his presentation, literature, and office. Over time, he branched out and started providing music and entertainment for other types of events.

It went on like this for several years. He would attend a seminar, do a show, and then heap praise on us at each follow-up dinner. His business was growing; he was thriving; and his Success Factor was moving in a positive direction.

You can imagine my surprise then when I received a phone call from him, and he said, "Chris, I know that you understand how much I appreciate everything you and your organization have done for me over the past six years, but frankly, I've worked so hard, for so long, that I've decided I need to change the way I'm doing business." He explained that he wanted to take some time off and establish policies and procedures that would allow him to spend more time at home with his young family. He wanted to step back from his business and work fewer hours. He had achieved an impressive level of success, and his existing clients were referring new business to him regularly. He felt he could do less advertising and enjoy some of the fruits of his labor without having an adverse impact on his business. He religiously captured referrals, and he followed up on everyone. Now, he was going to have his staff take some of the responsibility that he had shouldered and work less time. He felt he had earned it, so he was going to forfeit his booth in the two bridal shows that he had participated in. He was going to dedicate the funds to training his staff to follow-up on his free referrals.

Understand that during this period the Disneyland Hotel Bridal Show had a waiting list of over a hundred wedding professionals, who waited an average of 24 months to participate in the event. Sacrificing his booth in the show meant he would not be able to participate in the event again for quite some time. It was a very big deal to sacrifice your display space in the most successful show in the country.

We talked, and he appeared to understand his business. I couldn't deny that he was very successful, so I wished him well, reminded him that it had been my pleasure to serve him, and offered to work with him again if he ever wanted to do so. We gave him and his staff an open invitation to attend any seminars or Merchant Appreciation Dinners, encouraging him to stay in touch.

I didn't hear much from him for the next two years, and he did not participate in any bridal shows or wedding publications. On the few occasions I did see him at a mixer or networking event, it appeared as though his plan had worked well, and he was living life as he wanted.

Once again, I was surprised when he called one day and asked if we could get him into the next show. It seemed that while he had enjoyed the last couple of years, and he had been able to spend more time with his family, the referrals he had expected had not materialized and, in fact, had stopped coming in over the last year. His total number of weddings was down, so he was forced to raise prices to maintain his Success Level. This generated less business, and he was in a position that he now worked more time, stressing over his business, than he had two years before. He wanted back in the shows so that he could reduce his stress, not necessarily his hours.

It actually took six months to find a way to bring him back into the show, but once he returned, he was back on track. It didn't take long until he was once again generating a significant amount of business from the shows and the stress he had been facing dissipated. Nothing relieves stress like sales.

It's interesting to note that what happened to my good friend is that his Success Factor was so great that he decided it was time to enjoy some of the rewards that success brings. His mistake, however, was to do it in such a way that he took his eye off the ball and trimmed the successful things out of his business—obviously, the wrong things to give up.

My Balboa friend's mistakes:

- He stopped doing what was successful.
- He didn't have a sufficient plan.
- He had the wrong employees to back him up.
- He didn't have sufficient financial reserves.
- He overestimated his Success Factor.
- He didn't keep his head in the game.

What he did right:

- He learned from his mistakes.
- He reviewed his position and made adjustments.
- He returned to the fundamentals that built his business.

The Cake Lady

Even today, 15 years later, I smile when I think about this one. I have a long-time wedding cake designer who'd participated in both our bridal shows and our wedding magazine for a number of years. She is a wonderful woman, but no matter how hard she tried, it always appeared as though she was running behind.

At our bridal show, she had a great booth; it was very close to the main entrance. Even though we allowed our wedding professionals to move in for 12 hours the day before the show, she always seemed to show up 10 minutes before the show opened, and then tried to set up her booth. She was always tired because she'd been at Kinko's at 3 in the morning before the show having literature printed.

She was also one of the wedding professionals who attended the Merchant Maximizer Seminars on a regular basis. She had a basic understanding of what was important and what she should do at the bridal show. During the show, she always appeared to be doing whatever she could to be successful; she wasn't one of those wedding professionals who set up a booth and then disappear for eight hours. You never saw her standing around talking with the other vendors while brides came by her booth unassisted. After each event, she quickly contacted us and asked us to come see her to renew her booth space. We assumed she was a successful wedding cake designer. I did often wonder what type of follow-up she did after the show, because no matter what we discussed at the seminars, she always appeared to be very disorganized, which typically means that the wedding professional won't follow-up.

On one occasion, she called the office and asked if I could come to her place of business to renew her booth. I jumped in my car and drove the 60 miles to her Anaheim, California, business location. I was a little shocked and disheartened when I arrived at her store and realized as I walked in the front door, on a very hot day in August, that she had no power. The lights were off, display cases were unlit, and her coolers were getting hotter by the minute. Not wanting to be rude, I greeted her as usual and sat down to discuss the recent show with her. She said everything was fine, the show was great, and she was looking forward to renewing her booth in the upcoming January show. We talked easily for 20 or 30 minutes about the show and about life in general, but never once did I bring up the fact that we were sitting in a cake shop with no power. In the back of my mind, I thought she was going to ask me to hold her booth and let her pay a deposit later, but that didn't happen. As we were talking, she reached over on the counter, grabbed an envelope, and said, "Here's the deposit for the booth in cash. If you have your agreement, I'll OK it now." I pulled out an agreement, and she approved it. I gave her a copy and put my copy and the cash in my briefcase. At this point, she said, "Thanks for coming by."

I just couldn't keep it in any longer. I said, "I couldn't help but notice that you have no power. What's going on?"

She replied, "I spent so much money between the show, my staff, taxes, and some other expenses that I overdrew my checking account and couldn't pay the power bill. So they turned it off."

I couldn't believe what I was hearing. "Let me get this straight," I said, "you have no power, which means your display cases and your refrigerator don't work. Your customers are coming into a dark, hot location, yet you just gave me $600 cash as a deposit on a show that will be held in five months. I'm flattered, but confused."

She laughed and said, "I know it's strange, but I look at it this way. I'll have the power turned back on within a few days, and I have a friend who's helping me with my wedding cakes this weekend. I'm going to be inconvenienced for a few days, but if I lose my booth in your show, I'll lose business for the entire year. I can get by without power, but I can't get by without your show."

It was gratifying to listen to her, yet at the same time, it felt a little strange. Here's a lady who truly kept her head in the game. While she may be disorganized and needs to take a serious class to help her learn how to stay on task, she understands the importance of marketing her business, and she doesn't lose sight of the fact that if she changes what has been successful in the past, she very well may not be successful in the future.

My cake designer's mistakes:

- She's not organized.
- She's not serious about managing her money.
- She doesn't have a plan.

What my cake designer did right:

- She saw the big picture.
- She kept her head in the game.

Keeping your head in the game is instrumental to doubling your business in the next 12 months. We're going to lay out a plan that will take you step-by-step through what you have to do to increase your Success Factor and create the business of your dreams. Before we can do that, we need understand what the job really is.
What Is Your Job?

Think about it. Don't read forward yet; just think about what your primary job is within your organization.

I've asked presidents of companies, hourly employees, and part-time contract workers. As you might imagine, I've received a wide range of answers. I've been told, "I'm the president of the company; I make everything run." I've also been told, "I'm the catering manager, and without me, they wouldn't be able to have an event." In fact, I've been told just about everything you can possibly imagine at one time or another, but rarely, do people get the answer to this question correct.

There's one simple job that every person in the company has. You can be the janitor or you can be the president, and you still have this one responsibility to either the owners or the stockholders. It seems many companies have lost sight of the fact that this one primary job is more important than all others.

I believe that forgetting this primary job is why we have companies that are laying off thousands of people in an economic downturn. I'm amazed that some of the largest companies in the country, who profess to have unbelievable training programs and access to information that the average entrepreneur can only wish for, don't understand the basic principle that everybody has one primary job:

> **To sell product and make money for the company. The number one job for every employee is to be a salesperson before everything else.**

The next time you're interviewing job applicants, I want you to ask them one question. I don't care if they are applying to be a stock clerk, an accounting person, a human resource manager, or any position in your organization. I want you to ask them what their most important responsibility to the organization would be if you hired them.

If they don't say, "To sell product, increase profits, and create a better customer experience," don't hire them. They don't get it. There are people who seek out jobs within companies that are as far away from the sales department as possible. They say things like, "The reason I'm in accounting is I can't stand selling. I'll leave that to the Sales Department," or they say things like, "I hate high-pressure salespeople. I never want to be one." If they say that during an interview, don't hire them. If you hear this from existing employees, terminate them immediately. Show them the door and send them to the no-sales abyss that they long for. One reason virtually every government agency eventually becomes a sink hole of inefficiency is because of this type of attitude.

Let's take a look at the U.S. Postal Service. It announced it would lose up to $7 billion this year. It is in a severe budget shortfall. So how do the geniuses that run the postal service respond? Do they increase service, extend hours, create new opportunities, and make it easier for people to use their service? No, they want to do just the opposite. Their "must do" list includes:

- Raising rates
- Cutting hours
- Closing locations
- Cutting back on service

They simply don't get it. The reason the postal service is always losing money is that it has an inferior product that's overpriced and a staff of unionized, unmotivated people who don't work efficiently.

How does it expect more people to ship more mail if it closes offices, reduces service, and cuts hours? Only in the heads of government bureaucrats would this make sense. They have forgotten what their real job is. Every postal service employee should be tasked with increasing profits, selling product, and creating a better consumer experience. They need to find ways to be more efficient by dropping a bunch of the union rules and making it possible for people to do more than one job, and they need to reward employees based on performance. If they did that instead of worrying about the latest contract, they wouldn't be going bust, even with the growth of email.

In my organization, the simplest job every person has is to sell our product. Not all of them do it in a sales presentation, but all of them realize that their primary responsibility—the one that keeps us in business—is to sell our company or concept and our service to every qualified person they meet. If our accountants aren't proud enough of our service that they will sell it, then they don't belong here.

Every person who works for your company is a salesperson also. I understand that many of them don't actively participate in conducting sales presentations each day, but virtually everyone must market and promote your organization. The driver who delivers my dry cleaning to my front door is a salesperson for that business. Let's say there's a problem with my dry cleaning, and I say to him, "Excuse me, my last order was returned, and one of the shirts was still dirty." At that point, he becomes a salesperson trying to keep my business. Whether or not I continue to use his service is completely dependent upon how good a job he does solving the problem and selling me on the fact that it won't happen again. If he apologizes and fixes the problem in a professional manner, his boss is going to make money from me for years to come. If he acts disinterested or doesn't handle the problem appropriately, then the chances are that I'm going to stop using the service, and his boss is not going to get any more of my hard-earned money. This is why it's so crucial to make sure that everybody in your organization first understands that his or her job is to be a salesperson. They need to respect clients and handle every situation in an appropriate manner. Someone who specifically runs away from that responsibility is somebody who's going to do a bad job when you need them to step up. You need to go through your entire staff roster and eliminate anyone who isn't going to help you make money every day.

I understand this sounds harsh, and your first reaction may be, "I don't want to terminate them. I need to train them." Frankly, my first reaction would be to try to retrain them as well. What I've learned over the years, however, is that people who believe that sales is something they either can't do, don't want to do, or try to stay away from, cannot be trained to be professional salespeople. It's crucial to your organization that everybody be on the same page and understands that, first and foremost, they need to create income every day. If they're not creating income, they are dead weight, and you don't need them.

I also believe that many times it's the people who aren't immediately affiliated with the sales department who can be your best bird dogs for new business. For example, when someone calls your accounting person to discuss payment on a photography package, there should be incentives for your employee to discuss additional services and create up sales. Maybe the couple bought the $3,500 photography package, but as your person is talking to them about their payment, he or she notices that they didn't purchase a frame to go along with the 24 x 36 image that they've ordered. Many people in accounting would tell you that they don't feel comfortable suggesting additional product; after all, they are in accounting. That's wrong. Your accounting staff, your service personnel, and any employee who has contact with a customer should know that, first and foremost, their primary job is to make sales and profit for the company.

Many people, including business owners I've met, are comfortable saying things like, "I stay in the background, and I don't deal with the customers." Or, "I really don't like selling all that much, so I don't sell." The bottom line to advertising success is you have to be a salesperson, no matter who wants to tell you different.

We are all salespeople

CHAPTER 4 – Can We Talk?

As we've seen in the previous examples, people face a myriad challenges. We want to equip you with the information you need to be more successful. In order to do that, we need to establish a baseline or a way for us to set a standard that you will draw from as you move forward.

Much of the information we discuss here was taught to me by Tom Hopkins, a sales champion, whose books and tapes are required items for every one of my sales representatives. Over the years, we have taken much of Tom's basic information and adapted it to the wedding industry. I honestly can't point to any one technique that will move you from complete sales failure to complete sales success; it is a totality of the presentation that helps people achieve success. The old saying, "It's not where you started, but where you end up," is true when it comes to growing your business. We need to establish a common standard and standard terms so that we can have a significant degree of success along the way.

Definitions

Over the years, I've noted in many different sales courses and in working with different wedding-related businesses that each has its own terms and phraseology. In this book, we have very specific phrases that we'd like to use, and I want to be sure that as you read you have an understanding of the terms and phrases that will be used.

You can always use terms like deposit, contract, and pitch, and you will make some sales, but I firmly believe that by following a different path and using professional terminology designed to meet the client's expectations you will be more successful.

Lead

A lead is any live body that may need my product. It's very simple, anyone, anywhere who may need your product is a lead.

Contact

A contact is any live body that I contact.

Again this may seem very simple, but a contact for the purposes of the wedding professional is any live body you contact.

Appointment/Visit

An appointment is any live body I present my product to. The interesting thing about visiting with a bride today is that while it's usually best to have visits face-to-face, you can still visit with a bride-to-be without seeing the person. Now as we move forward and work on doubling our business, we're going to find that it is very important to meet face-to-face with as many people as we possibly can, but the definition of an appointment is anybody I present my product to. We're going to explain why we call them visits instead of appointments in a bit.

Sale

A sale has a little bit different definition than the others. My definition of a sale is any live <u>or dead body</u> that pays me for my product.

I'm not picky when it comes to selling product. If somebody who's passed on wants to buy my product, I'm going to sell it. This definition is not as simple as it may sound. For many business owners who employ salespeople, there's often a debate about what the sale is. In the business owner's mind, it is clear: The business owner believes that a sale occurs when a contract or agreement is turned in with an accompanying deposit or initial investment. If both an agreement and money are not received, it's not a sale.

In contrast, many salespeople like to call a successful appointment or contract, even without an initial investment a sale. How many times have you heard a salesperson say, "Well, I just got a great sale," and then, you find out sometime later that what they really meant was, "I just had a great visit, and I think it's going to be a sale someday." Some of the hardest working salespeople I've known have had a very hard time understanding the simple fact that it's not a sale until you have a written agreement or the client's deposit, which we call their initial investment.

Much of what you're going to be doing as you work to double your business over the next 12 months is to stop doing things the way you've done in the past. It's a fact that if you have not achieved the success you want over the last few years and you repeat exactly what you've been doing for the last two years, you're probably going to end up with the same results. So take a moment to not only understand the terms we're going to explain, but think through the reason why we use that verbiage. I understand that this may be a little uncomfortable. Whatever discomfort you have now will be more than offset by the feelings of success that you're going to feel 12 months from today.

Now that you know the general definitions, you need to know some basic techniques. The way you present yourself and your business matters, but did you know the very words you use can make or break a sale? Here are some additional terms that we use in our business that we have adopted after learning sales techniques taught by Tom Hopkins.

Buy vs. Own

People have a much harder time buying something than they do owning something. When you own something, you typically are willing to invest more in it.

Contract vs. Agreement

I believe that when you were working with a customer, whether you call them clients, customers, or another name, there is an awkward moment when you pull out the contract. As you'll learn later, when it's time for your office to secure an agreement with the customer, it's an easier transition and less formal when you don't call the paperwork a contract.

Sign vs. Approve

In order for your clients to invest in your service and own it, they need to approve the "paperwork." It's much less threatening than asking them to sign "the contract."

Pitch vs. Presentation

We never pitch our product. In fact, I hate the word "pitch" when it comes to sales. As a professional salesperson, I believe it cheapens what I do when it's called a pitch. And that's not what salespeople do anyhow. "Presentations" allow you to work with potential clients, discover what their needs are, and ensure that you have an opportunity to fill that need.

Professional presentations should be conducted with a track to run on. When I see wedding professionals talking to a client without using a brochure or some type of information to guide their presentation, I know that, in most cases, presentation isn't going to include all of the necessary information. A simple brochure, organized in such a way as to present the best features of your product, is the easiest way for you to be sure that each and every bride-to-be receives the same information.

Deposits vs. Initial Investment

We also do not take deposits. That doesn't mean that we don't require our clients to provide us with a form of payment when they secure services. We do in fact require every new client to make an initial investment for the services they requested. I'll admit, some of this seems like word games, and in some cases, it can become ridiculous as to what word you use or don't use. However, in the case of the word "deposit," that's not the case. As a wedding professional works with the bride-to-be, she wants to know that the person is going to help her create the wedding of her dreams. And I believe every wedding professional truly wants to help the bride-to-be do just that. Much of what we do as wedding professionals is perception before it is reality, and we want the bride to have the perception that her wedding is going to be exactly the way she has always envisioned it. Then we need to make that dream a reality.

I know that every wedding is going to have minor unscheduled challenges, but the competent wedding professional, particularly the wedding coordinator, will handle last-minute issues and problems in a way that the bride never sees, ensuring that she has the day she's always dreamed of.

It's important that from the very first time you start working with the bride-to-be that you stay on point and stay on message that you're helping her build the wedding of her dreams. To that end, the average bride is going to have some resistance to placing a deposit on her dream. However, that same bride won't have any concern about making an "initial investment" to ensure her dream comes true. That's why we always require an initial investment from our clients. We are forming a bond with them to ensure the success of whatever they're investing in. In the case of the bride, she's investing in her dream, and her initial investment is going to help her start down the road to making that dream come true.

Appointments vs. Visit

Don't you enjoy a visit more than you do an appointment? I always think of appointments as rigid, set periods that frankly don't sound very fun. You have an appointment with your dentist or doctor. You have an appointment with your attorney or accountant. You visit with your friends. Don't be put off by the fact that a visit seems more casual. You can still achieve a significant amount of sales success by having a track to run on when you visit with the bride-to-be.

Never forget, when the bride's dreams come true, so do yours—and you build your business. But who is the bride-to-be?

CHAPTER 5 – Who's Our Customer?

This seems like a simple enough question; as a wedding professional, it seems obvious who your customer is. You work with women who are about to be married. There's no need for an in-depth study or spending a lot of time looking into who your customer is because it's so obvious. But is it really that easy?

Look at any form of wedding advertising or attend any bridal show, and you will see a wide range of products and services available for the bride. Just as each form of advertising represents many different types of businesses, there are many different types of brides in the marketplace. It's important for wedding professionals to understand exactly what part of the wedding business is their niche.

For example, a recent study of brides indicated that more than 95 percent of all brides-to-be intend to hire a professional photographer, yet only 3 percent of them intended to even look at the option of having a butterfly release at their wedding. Knowing these facts, is it important for the photographer to understand that 9.5 out of every 10 brides intends to hire a professional photographer? You bet it is. The professional photographer can afford to be more selective in the weddings he chooses and the locations he services, while the professional butterfly-release people need to understand that 97 percent of the brides-to-be may not be interested in their message. Their job is to find those 3 people out of every 100 who want to hear about butterfly releases.

This is just one example of why the wedding professional must have a clear understanding of who their customer is. There are many different questions that could be asked about your current brides-to-be, and then that information must be recorded and tracked so that you can draw a very clear picture of your customer. Information that's important for you to know as you create your advertising program is:

Average age of your customers

- Size of average wedding held by your customers
- Average wedding investment of brides in your area
- Education level of your customers
- Average cost of competitive services in your area
- Size of wedding market in your area
- Percentage of market that is planning a wedding
- Percentage of the market that may need your service
- Average investment made by brides in your area for your type of service

These are just a few of the things that you need to know in order to create an effective advertising program. In truth, we could create a list hundreds of items long and still not cover all of the information that would be helpful in our analysis.

Not long ago, I had an opportunity to assist in the production of a major concert event on the West Coast. This event featured four massive stages and 75 bands, and it was spread throughout 350 acres of a national park. Over the two days of the concert, several thousand people attended the event. The average investment for a vendor to erect a tent and market to the concertgoers was $2,500. When the event was over and the vendors were moving out, I had an opportunity to meet a food vendor who specialized in vegan food.

This vendor was very angry and upset. It seems that after investing $2,500 in booth rental plus the cost of food, permits, equipment, and staffing, he had sold just over $2,000 in vegan food during the two days. He felt like the event was successful for many others, but it wasn't for him. He approached the show coordinator and asked about a refund of his display fees. Obviously, the coordinator wasn't receptive to a refund of fees, because she thought that if the event had been successful for many others, why would one display fail? Frankly, I felt the request was ridiculous. If you buy an ad in the newspaper, does it return your money if your ad is not as successful as you hoped?

In any event, I started thinking about our vegan friend. Why is it that his display didn't sell as much as he had hoped? When I returned to my office, I did a little research on vegan food. Until then, I wasn't very familiar with it. With just a 30-minute investment of time, I had the answer about why the exhibitor did so poorly, and honestly, I bet I knew more about vegan marketing than the vendor did. The reason he did poorly at the event is that he didn't know his customer. Here's why:

Consumers of vegan food represent just 2 percent of the population. Now, this doesn't mean that others would not try vegan food, but it does mean that only 2 percent of the population is exclusively vegan. At events where there are 20 to 30 other food vendors, you would need to offer something pretty incredible to get a person to switch from their preferred food to vegan food, especially if they are not dedicated vegan already. In a side-by-side contest of a hot dog vendor and a vegan vendor, the vegan vendor loses every time, even at events that are targeted toward healthy living and good food. What this means to our vegan friend is that the concert generated about 4,000 diners each day, with about 80 people who are dedicated vegans. Assuming not a single vegan selected food items from other food vendors, who may not have been dedicated vegan providers, but provided food a vegan would eat, his best possible outcome was 80 sales. With an average meal price of $10, he's looking at about $800 a day in sales, and this is a best-case scenario. Our vegan friend didn't stand a chance in a strictly side-by-side contest of food offerings. He may have increased his success if he had added an educational component to his presentation such as a "Try Vegan for the First Time" program, but based on a quick look at the numbers, he was doomed to failure with anything less than 25,000 people per day.

He didn't understand his market. And while after the event it's easy to yell at the promoter and complain, the bottom line is that he should have had a better plan and understood his market better. It's not up to the companies that sell advertising to look out for you. And while every salesperson wants you to believe he has your best interest at heart, there isn't much any advertising vendors will do after the fact if you're not successful—nor should they. It's your job to understand your business.

I also believe it's important to realize that you can go too far in the data research department. The average florist doesn't need to know the average length of time it takes a bride-to-be to go from her car to your front door, and while there are plenty of services and professionals who would love for you to hire them so that they could dazzle you with the information, it's probably not information that's going to help you with your business. I spent 30 minutes tops researching vegan food. It's important to have the right information without becoming bogged down in minutia.

You must strike a balance between the information that is useful and the information that isn't.

Complete this task:

List seven things that would make it easier for you to close every sale if you knew them before you met with the bride-to-be.

1. _____

2. _____

3. _____

4. _____

5. _____

6. _____

7. _____

The One Percent Rule

One important statistic that you need to know is what percentage of the market is getting married at any given time. In other words, when you purchase your advertising, what percentage of the audience is going to care about your message?

It's interesting to note that in the United States only about 1 percent of the population is actively planning a wedding at any given time. That means when you purchase advertising on the radio, 99 percent of the people who hear your message couldn't care less.

It's a daunting number when you think about it. In effect, you are throwing away 99 percent of the money you spend to reach your target market. You can increase the number of people who care about your message by picking advertising sources that attract the customers you want. Obviously, if you advertise in wedding magazines, bridal shows, wedding-related newspaper inserts, and other wedding-related advertising, a much higher percentage of the people that see that advertising are going to be interested in your message. But the fact of the matter remains that in radio, television, and, for the most part, newspaper, a large percentage of the audience who's going to see your message isn't going to care about it.

Finding That One Percent

So how best can you target that money so that you reach the widest audience? First, let's see where the bride-to-be spends her money. By glancing over some statistics about your customer, you can more easily see where and when advertising dollars would be well spent.

Wedding Statistics

- The average American engagement is 16 months.
- During the engagement period, couples buy:
- $4 billion in furniture
- $3 billion in house wares
- $400 million in tableware
- Each year 2.4 million weddings are performed in the U.S.
- Weddings are a $50 billion a year industry.
- Average age of first-time brides is 25.

- Average age of first-time groom is 27.5.
- On average, 175 guests are invited to a wedding.
- One-third of couples retain a wedding consultant.
- An average, honeymoon vacation is one week.
- Average income of a new couples is $60,000 per /year.
- Couples are waiting longer to get married.
- Tuxedoes are selected five to six months after the gown.
- Bridesmaids' gowns are selected three to four months in advance of wedding.
- Average size of wedding party is 12.
- Most brides (30 percent) plan their weddings in 7 to 12 months.
- 75 percent of brides receive a diamond engagement ring.
- 67 percent of repeat brides receive a diamond engagement ring.
- 15 percent of weddings include ethnic customs.
- 35 percent of weddings occur in the summer.
- 29 percent of weddings occur in the spring.
- 23 percent of weddings occur in the fall.
- 13 percent of weddings occur in the winter.
- 11 percent of winter weddings are Christmas weddings.

Wedding Costs

- $22,000 is the average spent on a traditional wedding.
- $72 billion is spent on weddings annually in the U.S.
- $19 billion is spent at wedding gift registries.
- The average amount spent on a bridal gown is $800.
- David's Bridal accounts for 20 percent of all bridal-gown sales.
- The average ring costs $2,000.

Top Wedding Destinations

- Las Vegas (100,000 weddings per/year)
- Hawaii (25,000 wedding per/year)

- Bahamas (5,000 weddings per/year)

Interesting Wedding Statistics

- 80 percent of traditional weddings are performed in churches or a synagogue.
- Four out of five brides are employed.
- There is a 43 percent chance of a marriage ending in divorce.
- 35 percent of brides and grooms have a valid passport.
- 64 percent of couples live together before marriage.
- 69 percent of couples know each other more than three years.
- 81 percent of brides will change their surnames.
- $93,750 is the approximate cost of the average Japanese wedding.
- 150,000 wedding ceremonies occurred in Canada in 2002.
- 53 percent of weddings occur in the afternoon.
- 31 percent of weddings occur in the evening.
- 16 percent of weddings occur in the morning.
- 30 percent of receptions are held in churches.
- 20 percent of receptions are held in hotels.
- 20 percent of receptions are held in country clubs.
- 38 percent of weddings have a buffet.
- 34 percent of weddings have a sit-down dinner.
- 28 percent of weddings serve only cake and punch.
- 62 percent of weddings have a flower girl.
- 56 percent have a ring bearer.
- Brides 18 to 39 receive 85 percent of all wedding cards.
- More than 4.2 million unmarried couples live together
- *Marriages by Month*
- January, 4.7%
- February, 7.0%
- March, 6.1%
- April, 7.4%
- May, 9.8%
- June, 10.8%
- July, 9.7%

- August, 10.2%
- September, 9.6%
- October, 9.4%
- November, 7.4%
- December, 7.8%
- *Wedding Costs by Category*
- Reception, 28.3%
- Consultant, 15.0% (if hired)
- Wedding rings, 11.5%
- Photography/video, 6.6%
- Bridal gown, 6.1%
- Music, 5.2%
- Flowers, 4.6%
- Bridal attendants' apparel, 4.5%
- Rehearsal dinner, 4.2%
- Men's formal wear, 3.2%
- Invitations, 2.8%
- Attendants' gifts, 2.1%
- Mother-of-the-bride apparel, 1.7%
- Bride's veil, 1.6%
- Clergy and ceremony fees, 1.2%
- Limousine, 0.9%
- Groom's attire, 0.8%

Honeymoon Statistics

Among couples who choose a traditional wedding:

- 99 percent take a honeymoon.
- Couples spend an average of $4,000 on their honeymoon. (That's three times as much as the average U.S. adult spends on a vacation.)
- The length of an average honeymoon is seven days.
- 45 percent of honeymoon trips are to domestic locations.
- 55 percent of honeymoon trips are to foreign locations.

- The honeymoon industry is a $12 billion a year industry.

Most Popular Honeymoon Activities

- Sightseeing, restaurants, entertainment, 75%
- Beaches and lakes, 45%
- Casinos, 20%
- Cruises, 15%
- Golf/sports vacations, 10%
- Skiing trips, 5%

Most Frequently Chosen Honeymoon Locations

- Aruba, 8%
- Bahamas, 20.2%
- Bermuda, 3.1%
- British Virgin Islands, 7%
- Caribbean, 34%
- Caribbean Islands, 6.3%
- The Cayman Islands, 10.5%
- Europe, 4%
- Hawaii, 33%
- Jamaica, 17.1%
- Mexico, 7%
- Puerto Rico, 3.8%
- St. Marten, 5.6%
- US Virgin Islands, 7%

Places to Stay While on a Honeymoon

- Hotel/motel, 46.1%
- Resort, 35.2%
- Boat/ship, 20.1%
- Bed and breakfast/inn, 8.2%
- Other, 8.9%

Transportation Used for Honeymoon

- Airplane, 76.2%
- Rental car, 60%
- Own car, 16.4%
- Boat/ship, 27%
- Railroad, 2.7%

Source: Association of Bridal Consultants, *Brides Magazine*, the US Census Bureau, and Chris Evans International.

As you can see, an enormous amount of money goes into the engagement, the wedding, and the honeymoon. All that planning has to start somewhere.

Where Does the Bride Start Planning?

John picks up Diane to go out to dinner. As she gets into the car and John closes the door for her, he runs around to the driver's side and tells her that they're going to a restaurant they wouldn't normally go to. Diane realizes that the restaurant is quite expensive, and in the back of her mind, she knows why. It's not until after dinner and just before dessert, when John drops to one knee in front of all the restaurant patrons and asks Diane to marry him, that she fully realizes what tonight is all about.

This scenario and similar scenes have happened millions of times for thousands of years. And as wedding professionals, we should all thank God every single day that although in today's world marriage may be a little muddled, it's still popular. The question we need to ask ourselves as wedding professionals is what will Diane be doing next? What will she do, and where will she go to plan her wedding? A firm understanding of bride's behaviors, while not 100 percent foolproof, will provide us with an edge on securing business from her.

Today, most wedding professionals agree that one of the first things a woman does after she gets engaged and officially becomes a bride-to-be, is visits the Internet to start perusing wedding services. A few short years ago, there was a general belief that the Internet would put many wedding professionals out of business. For the smart wedding professional who has learned how to capitalize on the Internet, the Web has proven to be a fantastic opportunity to reach out and find new business. For those who do not adjust with the times and learn to use the Web, there is a steep learning curve and, most likely, a decline in business.

Interestingly enough, this doesn't mean that Diane is going to plan all of her wedding online. As a source of information, the Internet can't be beat. You can Google more information about planning a wedding in an evening than if you read every wedding planning guide you could get your hands on. But actually booking services and dealing with wedding professionals still remains, for the most part, a one-on-one activity that Diane is going to want to do face-to-face with wedding professionals.

We know statistically that there are six steps Diane will take as she starts to plan her wedding. While the order that these occur in is not always the same, for the most part, most brides do the following:

- Visit the Internet for information (90%)
- Purchase a wedding magazine (86%)
- Start planning with her mother (68%)
- Start planning with her girlfriends (21%)
- Register with at least one major retailer (58%)
- Attend a bridal show (49%)

Understanding some of the first steps that Diane will take will allow us to be more proactive and make sure that we capitalize on the opportunities that present themselves as she moves forward.

No amount of research about the bride is going to help wedding professionals who don't understand what the bride wants and how their service can help her have the wedding of her dreams. No matter how automated our Internet-based society becomes, the simple fact remains that most first-time brides pictures themselves as princesses, and the grooms are knights in shining armor. Wedding professionals who can tap into this emotion, feed the fantasy, and provide great service are the ones who will garner most of the business.

CHAPTER 6 – What Do You Really Want?

For years, it has been drilled into business owners that they must advertise to secure customers; after all, it takes money to make money right?

That makes perfect sense if you have money to begin with, but what do you do if you don't have money to start advertising or, worse yet, you've spent all your money on advertising that didn't work? In fact, more often than not, the wedding professionals I've spoken with can provide a long list of advertising that didn't work and a very short list of the advertising that did.

In the 23 years I have worked in the wedding business, my experience is that wedding professionals have a limited advertising budget to work with, and every dollar they spend must yield significant results. The first reaction they have to an unsuccessful advertising campaign is to cut their advertising dollars and try to ride out the storm. With a limited budget, what more can they do?

Obviously, the answer to this dilemma is to ensure that you don't have an unsuccessful advertising campaign. I'll admit that's easier said than done, but there are a number of steps you can take to make the most unsuccessful form of advertising work.

Let's start with a core belief that I hold: I believe the vast majority of wedding professionals are hard working individuals who love what they do, and most of them that I've come to know are good at what they do. They work long hours to make sure every bride-to-be receives the finest service they can provide, and for the most part, they deliver. Any wedding professional who's been in business for any length of time can show you a long list of happy clients, so clearly they have the ability to deliver great product.

However, a long list of happy customers and a love for what you do won't do a thing to help your advertising campaigns work.

Think about it. When is the last time you walked out of a bridal show with more business than you could handle? The attendance may have been great, and you may have met hundreds of brides-to-be. However, in most cases, when you break down your booth and pack-up to go home, you have no idea if the show was successful for you.

You can carry this through to many other forms of advertising. When was the last time you received more business than you expected from a wedding publication? How about an online service?

In fact, when is the last time you had any measurable response to any type of advertising? My experience has taught me most wedding professionals don't get the response they want to advertising because they don't know what they want. Let me reiterate: While many forms of advertising may work, many wedding professionals would never know it, because they have no clue what they want out of advertising.

During my seminars, "How to Double Your Wedding Business in the Next 12 Months'" I ask this question: Why do bridal businesses advertise? The answers typically run like this:

- To get leads
- To generate interest in my product
- To build credibility
- To educate about my services
- To get the word out

Eventually, someone will say: "To make sales!"—and then they get a prize! When did it become fashionable to spend hundreds, maybe thousands, of dollars to get leads or generate interest in a product? Why does a wedding professional need to invest in getting the word out? The problem I see over and over again is that most of these professionals do not understand the most important rule in running a business.

This brings us to our first "Evans Truism". Evans Truisms are strikingly intelligent bits of wisdom you must agree with before you are allowed to move forward and read the rest of the book. My first truism is this:

- **The amount of money I put in my checking account is directly related to the number of sales I make.**

Startling isn't it? Do you agree? I'm serious; people sometimes want to debate this simple point. They will say things like, "If I make one big sale with 80 percent profit margin and 10 small sales with 10 percent margin, your truism is not true." At that point, I generally ask them to leave, because they just don't get it. Answer these questions:

> Would you rather have 10,000 people hear about your business or 10 people buy your product?

> Would you rather have the most beautiful double page spread in the bridal magazine or five sales?

> If you had your choice between doing wedding advice on a weekly television show or spending the same time on the phone to secure three new clients, which would you choose?

Many wedding professionals go for the splashiest opportunity that reaches the most people and provides the most *ego gratification,* even if it doesn't generate sales. Then, when no sales come in, the wedding professional defaults to that old lament: "It should have brought in business."

The fact is that most wedding professionals do not have a clearly defined idea of what they want. They understand they must generate more income than they have in expenses, but many cannot begin to define what that amount would be. If you can't identify what you want, there is no way you can expect an advertising provider to fill your needs. It's like a bride coming to a florist and saying, "I want nice flowers." The florist delivers flowers, believing they are the best flowers ever arranged, only to have the bride be bitterly disappointed, because they aren't what she expected.

You must have a clear idea of what you want your advertising to do. You must have a clear and measurable goal for every piece of advertising you commit to and a goal about what the advertising should achieve. The goal must be realistic. Placing an ad in the Yellow Pages and expecting 25 calls a day may not be realistic. In fact, 25 calls in six months may not be realistic for some types of wedding professionals.

Your advertising goal may change with each form of advertising. When you participate in a bridal show, your goal may be to secure face-to-face visits, but when you advertise in a wedding magazine, the goal may be to generate incoming calls. It's not as important what the goal is, as it is to have a clearly defined goal. Of course, if you don't have enough advertising designed to generate sales, the other goals are moot.

Take a moment and list your primary goal for each of the following forms of advertising:

Radio - _____

TV - _____

Phone Book - _____

Magazine - _____

Newspaper - _____

Web - _____

Direct Mail - _____

Bridal Show - _____

Once you have a primary goal, it's easier to set up a plan to meet that goal.

Take a moment and decide what the primary reason is that you advertise your business. Of all the great things advertising can do for you, what is the most important? If, like me, your goal is to sell more products and earn more profit, read on!

Why Are You in the Wedding Business?

Chances are, you came to the wedding industry by accident. Many of the best wedding professionals have—for example, like the expert caterer who just likes to cook and found out that weddings are a great way to keep the lights on, or the DJ who enjoys music and decided to work at weddings on weekends to cover the cost of new equipment.

Then there are the wedding planners. Most of the wedding planners I know decided to get into the business after their sister's wedding, their wedding, or their daughter's wedding. They found that, while helping someone else plan a wedding, they had a great time; it truly is fun to plan such a celebration.

It doesn't matter how you came to the wedding business, by accident or by plan, we call it business for a reason. You have to understand that while we all enjoy working with brides, it is work. There is a level of professionalism and expertise you have to master to stay in the business. We have all heard stories of the photographers or wedding providers who didn't show up for a wedding or closed their business just before a bride's wedding date. Unfortunately, these things happen, but the primary goal of any wedding professional should be to deliver a quality product. That's why it's important to identify why you are in the wedding business. What is the reason you get up every day and work in the industry?

Take a moment and write down three reasons why you do what you do. It will provide clarity and give us a base to work from.

The three reasons I'm in the wedding business are...

1._____

2._____

3. _____

My Story – Part 2

Going back to my first experience as a video vendor at a bridal show... As I stood in the dark watching gown after gown float by on the fashion show stage, my first reaction was to get angry. After all, I paid as much as a bridal shop to be there, and while I knew the shop had additional costs, such as staff, gowns, and wear and tear on the dresses, all was offset nicely by the fact they had one-on-one exposure to every bride for an hour. I had two or three minutes with each bride—tops!

It didn't take long to realize no matter how unfair I believed it was; nothing was going to change. First, a bridal shop owner and a tux shop owner ran the bridal association producing the show. And, taking a quick look at the smiling faces of the brides as they watched the gowns on stage, I knew that short of an explosion, I wasn't going to get equal time. I would have to play with the cards I was dealt.

I had to develop a plan that allowed me to have some type of impact and capture the business in a very short time frame. That's why we developed the system I explained in the beginning of this book: We took a free portrait of the bride-to-be at the show and delivered it in a few days. The portrait was simply a 5x7 picture of the bride-to-be, usually in street clothes so that it didn't interfere with any professional photographers at the event. I could have an entire roll of film proofed to 5x7 for about $15, and the delivery was an excellent way to meet the bride at her home.

I know some of you are cringing at the thought of calling on brides in their homes. It seems so inefficient and outdated, and that may be quite true in some parts of the country. However, in many parts of America, wedding professionals meet one-on-one in the homes of clients every day. It may not be an efficient use of your time to travel from Ventura, California, to a face-to-face visit in Anaheim, over 90 miles away, but what's the down side to meeting a local bride-to-be in her home? It's not high tech. It's not fancy. But, it is a great way to find the bride's needs and fill them.

As my wedding business grew, I met many people involved in the video production business. It always made me smile to find out that the professional video people at the television stations were interested in making money by shooting weddings on weekends, and the few wedding videographers I knew all wanted to do professional productions on weekdays.

Eventually, I had an opportunity to manage a video-editing facility that was newly opened. An investor thought that having an editing studio available for anyone to rent would be a good investment, and I had access to thousands of dollars worth of editing equipment. It was a win-win situation that was soon to change.

My wife was looking through the newspaper and noticed a help wanted ad for Fisher Electronics, which had just been purchased by Sanyo Electronics. Fisher needed a representative with video background to represent its product in the Central Valley of California. At first, I wasn't very interested. However, one thing I have learned is that my wife has great instincts, so I dutifully followed her suggestion and called the telephone number listed in the want ad. It was obvious I was talking to a person who had received a ton of resumes for the position. At one point, he said, "Just send your resume over to me, and I'll put it in the stack." I half jokingly said, "No, I don't want my resume to go in the stack. I want to deliver it in person. What's the best time to bring it by tomorrow morning or afternoon?" He said, "We're in San Francisco, so just mail it." I said, "I really want to drop it by and meet you. What time tomorrow should I do that?" There was a pause, and he said, "You're in Fresno. You're four hours away." To which, I replied, "That is true." He said, "OK. Meet me here in the office at 9 a.m. and don't be late." After saying thanks, I hung up.

It suddenly hit me that, I had just committed to deliver a resume four hours away from home at 9 o'clock the next morning. Traffic would add another two hours; I would have to leave my home at 3 a.m. I had no intention of doing that. Who would be crazy enough to drive six hours, halfway across California, just to deliver a resume? I told my wife I wasn't going.

The alarm went off at 2:30 a.m. Even though I had only slept about two hours, I shot up, grabbed a quick shower, and started driving to San Francisco. I arrived at the Fisher/Sanyo office at 8:45 and checked in at the front desk. At about 9:20, the receptionist asked me, "Who are you here to see again?" I gave her the name for the third time. "I don't think he's in today," she said.

At just about that time, a gentleman walked in the front door. The receptionist looked surprised and told him, "Your 9 a.m. appointment is here." He looked at me saying, "You showed up; I didn't expect to see you. Come on back. I've got 10 minutes for you." Two hours later, I asked my new friend Ed, "Do you want me to start calling on accounts right away, or is there some training you would like me to go through?" He smiled and said, "As much as I want to hire you, I have a representative in Sacramento who will lose part of his territory if you come on board. I need you to meet with him and make sure it's a good fit, because the two of you will be working together. Give me a week, and I'll set up a meeting for you to meet."

At this point, I had been up since 2:30 a.m. Ed was late for our appointment, and now he wanted to blow me off for a week! I just wasn't in the mood. I said, "Ed, I have to drive back to Fresno, and I can go through Firebaugh, or I can cut across and hit Sacramento before going south to Fresno. Let's set-up a dinner appointment with your rep, and I'll meet him today." Ed smiled at me, called me a pushy S.O.B., picked up his phone, and called the rep. We had a great dinner, and became good friends. I started work the next week. I just had to go through some training in Los Angeles before I could start calling on accounts.

Before I move on to what happened in Los Angeles, I want to share one interesting fact. When I talked to Ed in his office on the first day, he showed me the stack of resumes he had received. As I looked at some of the resumes of the people whose employment hopes I was trying to squash, I came across two resumes from people I knew in Fresno. In fact, one of the people was a very good friend. I did have a second of guilt about taking a job my friend wanted, but then again, if he had truly wanted this job, he could have gone out of his way to stand out from the crowd.

As a wedding professional, you may have friendly competitors in this business. You absolutely must be willing to do whatever you can that is legal, ethical, and moral to bring in as much business as possible to your company. I was once told that Walt Disney said, while looking out over a crowd at Disneyland, "Look at all the people, and every one of them has my money in their pockets." I haven't verified he ever really said that, but it is a great thought. Every bride-to-be you meet has your money in her pocket! You need to create enough desire for her to give you your money.

I arrived in Los Angeles at the Century Plaza Hotel late in the afternoon about a week after my first meeting with Ed. The best part of working for Fisher was everything it did, it did first class. Over the next three days, I went through some of the best sales training I have ever experienced. I could write a book about this one experience. The bottom line was after three days of training with the corporate headquarters, I was asked to transfer to Southern California and become the national sales trainer for Fisher Electronics.

A little over a week earlier, I was as happy as a clam, videotaping weddings and living in Fresno. Now I had a decision to make. Keep doing what I had been doing, or give it up and take a management position with a world-class company as one of the 13 U.S.-based managers who ran the billion-dollar company. Even though there always seemed to be tension between the U.S. managers and their Japanese counterparts, it was a once in a lifetime opportunity, which never would have happened if I had let my resume go into a stack on Ed's desk.

In less than a month, I sold Video Pro, stopped managing the editing bay, sold our home, and we moved to Thousand Oaks, California, where every dime we had made from our home sale in Fresno barely covered the deposit on the new home we were renting. Our rental in Thousand Oaks wasn't going to be ready for 90 days, so we moved in with my parents. I commuted 85 miles each way, morning and night, until we could move in. It was a very hectic time, but in the end, I was the national training manager for a world-class manufacturer of consumer electronics. I had a dream job that offered great pay, fantastic perks, and superb travel opportunities. I planned on staying with Fisher for the rest of my life. Bridal shows and videotaping was something I had enjoyed, but I would never do again—or so I thought.

To be continued…

CHAPTER 7 – How Do We Advertise?

In the first few chapters of this book, we promised to address one of the big questions that made you pick up the book in the first place:

➢ Why hasn't my advertising worked?

You may be thinking, "I've spent thousands of dollars to get my name and contact information in the hands of the bride-to-be, yet nothing seems to have returned the investment." Don't feel like you're all alone. I've met thousands of wedding professionals who have the same complaint. Most tried many different forms of advertising, yet what they purchased rarely delivered anything like the return they expected. To be fair, there are some important rules of advertising that many wedding professionals violate.

The Most Important Rule of Selling

Can you tell me the most important rule of selling? I ask this question at each seminar and training program I host. Hands will shoot up all over the room, and people will start yelling answers, which we then write on a whiteboard in the front. It's not uncommon to have answers like:

- You need to know your product.
- You need to believe in what you sell.
- You must have a quality product.
- You must fill the client's needs.
- You need to listen to the customer.
- You need to put yourself in the customer's shoes.

Knowing your product and believing in what you sell is very important. Moreover, who among us wants to represent a product that isn't top quality or the client doesn't need. Nevertheless, in our case, because you are a wedding professional, I'm assuming you have a good product, and you believe in what you're selling. In addition, I don't believe most wedding professionals will sell the bride something she doesn't need.

You could have a lousy product you don't know anything about, that the client doesn't need, and you would still need someone to sell to in order to push the lousy product. It's simple; no prospects equals no sales.

I believe the most important rule of selling is:

You Must Have Someone to Sell To

What good is having the world's best flowers or wedding entertainment if you don't have someone to experience it? You need to have a steady stream of warm bodies to tell about your product, or it doesn't matter how good your product or service is. You will be out of business.

I find that many wedding professionals delegate the most important part of their business to others. Most of them will readily acknowledge that prospecting and finding potential customers is one of the primary duties they have, yet they delegate it to others.

They invest in things like the Yellow Pages, wedding magazine ads, newspaper ads, radio advertising, and every other advertising they can purchase, while they are busy working on less important facets of their business, such as Myspace and Facebook or cleaning the office. Part of the problem is traditional forms of advertising have worked in the past, so most wedding professionals believe they will work for them now. I understand telephoning 200 prospective customers is harder than designing and placing a newspaper ad that will reach 80,000 people, but as we will see, the ad is typically not half as effective. While advertisers will often tout how cost effective their advertising is, we want to focus on results and not on the lowest cost per thousand impressions.

It's clear; the most important rule of selling for most wedding professionals is you must have someone to sell too. A little later in the book, we are going to explore all advertising methods we use in an attempt to find new brides to sell to, and we're going to discover what works and what doesn't.

You Must Track Your Advertising Responses

We all know if you're going to invest money in advertising you have to have some way to track the results. But, many times, I find wedding professionals don't have a solid system that allows them to know where their business comes from. It's like taking a dart and throwing it at a board full of balloons in the dark. You'll probably hit something, but you won't know what you hit or where it came from if you don't have a way to track your responses.

Every interaction with a potential customer should be preceded by an inquiry into how they heard about your product or service. That information should be tracked on an advertising response worksheet—a simple chart of the advertising you are participating in, the response you expect, and then, the actual number of responses. You can review a copy of the sheet I recommend in the companion workbook.

There are a few additional easy-to-follow rules that you should follow regardless of the advertising you invest in.

You Must Make an Offer

It's important to make an offer in your advertising. However, this doesn't mean your ad should scream out, "SAVE $500!" While saving $500 is good, there are many other offers you can make that don't cut into your bottom-line profit. I have seen thousands of offers that wedding professionals have made in their advertising. Some of the most tired and ineffective offers are:

- Free engagement portrait
- Free engagement sitting
- Three day trip to anywhere (Las Vegas, Hawaii, Bahamas, etc.)
- Free ring cleaning
- Free hors d'oeuvres
- Save money

Tired, old offers don't do a thing to help you build business. Some new, fresh offers that may seem more appealing to the bride-to-be are:

- Free wedding webpage
- Free digital download of images
- Free airfare
- Lifetime jewelry tune-ups

In the year 2000, we told wedding professionals they had to update their 1980's thinking and get up to speed. Today, you need to replace last month's thinking to stay ahead of the competition. If there ever was a time to think outside the box, it is now!

You Must Advertise Consistently

Some wedding professionals will invest in one advertisement, not track their results, not make an offer, and then cancel future advertising, because it didn't work. The truth of the matter is this: the advertising may have worked well. The problem was the wedding professionals didn't work.

Advertising is not a one-time investment. The reason you see major companies advertising every day on television, radio, and newspaper is they understand that consistently reminding their potential customers they are available to fill their needs is beneficial. As a wedding professional, you may not have the financial resources to invest in advertising to build your brand. This simply means you need to be very selective and only use advertising that delivers the greatest return. If you're on a limited budget and your goal is to visit with brides face-to-face, select the form of advertising that delivers the highest percentage of face-to-face visits. Later, as your budget grows, you can add additional advertising to build name awareness and brand recognition.

One advertising failure is simply that. One way of advertising didn't work. Canceling your advertising because you didn't get the response you wanted makes about as much sense as selling your car because you are low on gas. Simply refill the tank and move on.

Use Third Party Influence when Possible

It's one thing to tell the bride you're good at something, but there is a completely different level of credibility when someone else tells them you are the world's best.

Find an informational and credibility building organization and participate in their programs. For years, companies like the Better Business Bureau or your local Chamber of Commerce have been good, third party, credibly boosters. Recently, Certified Wedding Pros.com has been able to capture the desire of the bride to find certified wedding professionals while offering wedding professionals an opportunity to establish themselves as credibility experts.

Information about Certified wedding professionals can be found at www.CertifiedWeddingPros.com

CHAPTER 8 – How Well Does Advertising Perform?

Advertising Rankings

Let's take a quick look at each form of advertising and establish how effective each is. We are going to discuss each type of advertising and then rank it in the following areas:

- Effectiveness
- Cost
- Core market reach
- Return on investment

Effectiveness of Your Advertising

Effectiveness is the advertising's ability to present your message to the bride-to-be in a manner that allows you to benefit. A small Yellow Pages ad is going to be less effective than a wedding magazine ad.

Cost

Cost is the amount of money required to create an effective advertising message.

Core Market Reach

Core market reach represents a ranking based on the number of qualified brides-to-be who receive your message. Radio reaches the masses, but a bridal show reaches more qualified prospects. Thus, it will rank higher.

Return on Investment

Return on Investment is a ranking based on the overall sales you can expect from the advertising investment.

Newspapers

It's appropriate that we should start our analysis of advertising with newspapers. In the early 1600s, the first newspaper on this continent only lasted a few short years until the editor was arrested and put in jail, because the king didn't endorse it.

In many ways, the newspaper has remained the same since that time. It is simply a daily compilation of news and commentary that people read to keep informed with current events. Open any newspaper and you will find a wide range of advertising from many different businesses.

The first thing we have to determine as we look at the newspaper is who reads the newspaper? Does the bride-to-be routinely read one? Call your local newspaper office and request a media kit. Look over the demographics of their readership (as you get past the fact that every newspaper has the most-affluent readers and every newspaper has the biggest circulation), and you will find there is a huge gap in the readership. That gap exists in the unmarried, 18 - 28 year-old female demographic.

Women in this age group statistically do not read the newspaper as often as married women, older women, or any male age group. I've never met a person in newspaper advertising who would refuse to take my advertising dollars. Typically, they will counsel me to place my advertisement near the movies section or in their weekend calendar section or any one of the many sections of the newspaper the publishers have created to generate more advertising revenue. But, the fact of the matter is, it doesn't matter where I place my ad. If my target customer isn't reading the newspaper, I won't have good results.

Many papers have developed their own wedding insert, which they produce once or twice a year. Typically, the wedding insert will feature a wonderful picture of a bride on the cover and then several pages of advertising, featuring a wide range of wedding related services. My experience has been that while the wedding sections produced by newspapers do generate a significant increase in wedding advertising revenue for the newspaper, they're not always beneficial for the wedding professional.

Let's analyze the newspaper-wedding insert for a minute. Simply because the newspaper produces a section that contains page after page of advertising and articles about planning your wedding does not mean the 18 to 28-year-old female, who's not reading the paper, will purchase the paper the day it is published.

It's unlikely the bride-to-be who does not normally read the paper will know there's going to be a wedding insert on Sunday. Newspapers don't put the insert on the outside of the paper, so brides won't see it in the new rack. However, it doesn't mean there is no value to the wedding insert in the newspaper. It simply means you have to understand what value it has, if any.

Who does read the newspaper, and who will most likely see the wedding insert? The mother of the bride, that's who. Is it a good investment to place your advertising in a wedding insert to reach the mother of the bride? If you believe it is, by all means, do it. Remember, once the mother of the bride takes the wedding insert and gives it to the bride, the bride must then read through it and respond to your ad, so your message must stand out from the others. You need to motivate the bride-to-be to contact you. Later, we're going to speak about advertising design and what you can do to make your message pop. This is truly a case where if you don't have a message that stands out from the rest, it's going to be very hard for you to recoup your investment. More recently, newspapers have been doing everything in their power to get the public to log on to their web page. As many newspapers close down, editors are scrambling to find a way to compete with all the other advertising. Unfortunately, most newspapers' websites are nothing more than lame rewrites of their newspapers. Sure, they have an opportunity to earn some extra revenue by selling you a web link, but when you look at the demographics of who visits their web pages, it still doesn't make sense for the average wedding professional. After all, if a bride-to-be doesn't read the newspaper, what motivation would she have to log onto the newspapers web page? I guess the newspapers haven't heard about Google, Yahoo, Myspace, and Facebook.

Newspaper Effectiveness Ranking

- Effectiveness   2
- Cost   1
- Core market reach   1
- Return on investment   1

OVERALL RANKING   1.25 – F

Magazines

I love wedding magazines, and so do the brides. Statistics show one of the first purchases the brides-to-be make after becoming engaged is a wedding magazine. I envision dreamy-eyed women, sitting at home, perusing the pages of the wedding magazine for hours on end. For the most part, that image is probably accurate. Brides love to look at wedding magazines.

Does that mean that your advertising investment in the magazine makes sense?

Wedding magazines come in all shapes and sizes. There are full-size magazines that you can purchase in grocery stores, drug stores, and bookstores. There are the pocket directories that you pick up for free at wedding businesses. Smaller publications rely on a network of wedding professionals to handle their magazines, while the larger national magazines are distributed through magazine racks and retail stores.

Many local publications will charge less than the national publications overall, but on a cost-per-thousand basis, they are far more expensive. I believe an investment of more than a few hundred dollars in a local publication would not be effective.

Simply because a company has the ability to produce a pocket size wedding directory and distribute it through local bridal retailers, doesn't mean your message is reaching brides effectively. If a local publication has 25 vendors distributing its magazine, and each local vendor has 15 brides a week visit its business, you have just 375 copies of the magazine being handed out each week. With such limited circulation, there's no way to create the reach that it would take for the average local wedding publication to warrant a higher investment.

My point isn't that all local wedding directories are bad or do not deserve your consideration. However, I do believe when it comes time to determine the best return on your advertising investment, local bridal publications yield a much lower response and produce fewer face-to-face opportunities than other advertising media.

All publishers rely on their circulation number to justify the price of their advertising. They will tell you that because they produced 25,000 copies of their magazine, they offer incredible reach. Yet as we discussed earlier, the sheer fact that many copies of a publication are produced does not translate into a substantial number of brides finding your information.

One interesting statistic quoted by magazine publishers is the pass along rate. Typically, the pass along rate is two or three times more than the circulation. A pass along rate three times more than circulation means each magazine distributed is read by twice as many people as those who originally acquired it. When you analyze how the pass along rate is derived, you see how absurd it really is.

<u>Magazine Effectiveness Ranking</u>

- Effectiveness   2
- Cost   3
- Core market reach   10
- Return on investment   2

OVERALL RANKING   4.2 –C

Radio / Television

There are many different radio and television advertising opportunities for the wedding professional, and your choices are growing every day. Twenty years ago most homes in the United States had just three channels to choose from, but over time, there's been extreme growth in the number of television and radio stations in each market.

Without a doubt, television and radio are the best outlets for reaching large numbers of people with your advertising message. That doesn't mean, however, that television and radio are the best use of your advertising dollar.

You can reach more people faster by using the proper television or radio station. That's why radio and television advertising are typically the most expensive promotions you can invest in. When you consider all of the costs associated with a TV commercial, including the production costs, the costs of airing the commercial, and the challenge of finding the right channel and right time to broadcast your message, it's easy to see how many wedding professionals find that they don't even cover their costs.

Today, it's hard to isolate what channel the bride-to-be is watching and when she's watching it. Even when you find cable channels that have shows specifically about planning a wedding, it doesn't guarantee a significant return on your investment. Let's use our hometown as an example.

We live and work in Moorpark, California. Moorpark is a bedroom community located in Ventura County, approximately 50 miles from downtown Los Angeles. The population is a little over 35,000 people. Statistically, we know that Moorpark should generate about 350 weddings each year, which we can average out to about 30 per month. Moorpark has cable television provided by Time Warner Cable, which offers about 300 television channels.

Time Warner offers many advertising packages for businesses. You can run a commercial on any one of the 300 stations, and ad reps are happy to point you towards shows that are watched by women ages 18 to 28. Before we can even begin to assess what our frequency or reach should be for any given cable TV station, however, we have to determine what time slot we want to advertise in. Typically, the local cable or radio station will provide you with data on how many people watch each show. Lately, many of the smaller stations have started using their own numbers instead of a reputable rating service such as Arbitron. If you ask for the Arbitron statistics, they will say something like, "We found that in this market, Arbitron doesn't truly reflect the numbers, so we've chosen to participate in a different rating service." This could be the first red flag you run into when purchasing radio or TV advertising. While many agree that Arbitron doesn't accurately reflect every single market in the country, a station's resistance to participating in what is typically considered to be the gold standard of advertiser rankings would cause me to wonder about the veracity of its numbers.

Let's look at it this way. The bride-to-be typically watches somewhere between three and five hours of TV a day. If the woman lives in Moorpark, she can watch any one of 300 different television stations during that five-hour time frame. What are the chances that any sizable numbers of the 30 brides who represent the total number of brides available each month are going to watch the one or two stations you pick out of the 300 that are offered? Now, I understand some wedding shows are more likely to be watched by brides-to-be, which is good, but I think you see the problem we have.

Some cable shows may have only 10 or 15 viewers, total. While you may be able to buy cable TV advertising for as little as $10 or $15 per commercial, does it really make sense to throw away $15 if nobody's receiving your message?

You can clearly see that while television and radio can put your message in front of many people quickly, it's very possible that the people who see your message will have no interest whatsoever in it.

To combat that problem, most television and radio stations will put together a program for you that they call a T.A.P. program. T.A.P. stands for Total Audience Participation. Sometimes, they call it a Rotator. No matter what they call it, the general program provides you with a set number of commercials spread out over a one-week period. The commercials rotate time frames so that you never have your advertising run during the same time each day.

For example, if your commercial runs at 8 a.m. on Monday, it would run at noon on Tuesday and maybe at 3 o'clock on Wednesday. That way, you have an opportunity to have your commercial viewed by as many different people as possible. With a program like this, you will typically run three to four commercials a day for a week. With every commercial playing at a different time each day, you are reaching a large percentage of the viewing audience.

As we've already discussed, frequency is very important, yet the T.A.P. program provides exactly the opposite. It provides significant reach, because you are reaching many different parts of the viewing audience, but it provides little, if any, frequency. As a wedding professional, frequency is one of the most important elements of your advertising, and these short run schedules typically don't work. One thing that a T.A.P. program does provide is an opportunity for the advertising outlet to smooth out its advertising sales and sell commercial time slots that typically are harder to sell. Other than infomercials, few, if any, advertisers benefit from running commercials between midnight and 6 a.m.

To be sure, there is an opportunity to make radio and television work for your business. However, when you purchase this form of advertising, you have to be aware of what results to expect and, more importantly, what to do with those results. Just as with many other things in life, you get what you pay for.

Typically, if you are buying television advertising on a cable station for $25 per commercial, you're not going to receive good results. This was clear to us many years ago when we were advertising a bridal show at the Disneyland Hotel. We had an opportunity to buy many different cable TV stations and radio. We met with an advertising consultant and reviewed the available data. When we were done analyzing all the information, we determined it was better for us to purchase 10-second television commercials on the major networks than it was to use cable outlets.

At the time, NBC charged $5,000 for each 10-second spot during *The Tonight Show with Johnny Carson*. The cable network offered more than 150 commercials on its various stations for the same $5,000. We wanted as many people as possible to hear our message, and we hoped they would call our 800 number and order tickets to the show. This was before the Internet, and we had six operators sitting in our office at 11:30 p.m. awaiting callers from those 10-second TV commercials.

It was amazing. The minute the television commercial ran, the phones would light up. And to show you how frequency works, our experience was typically this: On the first night, the phones would ring for about 20 minutes. On the second night, we ran the same 10-second commercial during the same time slot, and the phones would ring for about 30 minutes. By the third night, the phones would ring consistently for an hour. Now this is at 11:30 p.m., and the phones would ring for one hour! When we were fortunate enough to have the money to purchase a fourth or fifth night of advertising, not only would the phones ring most of the night, they would ring the next day as well. During one of our most successful campaigns, we had advanced ticket sales of 1,520 before the show opened. We had invested $20,000 in television and generated $10,600 in ticket sales. By most standards, that would be a failure, but for us, it was success. Obviously, a bridal show promoter wants to know that people are coming to the show. We may not have a cost of goods per se, but we do need to invest to make sure engaged women are at the event.

In this case, I have no doubt that if we had spent $20,000 on cable television and ran 600 commercials, we would not have received one-tenth of the ticket sales we did by using network television. You get what you pay for.

Radio / Television Effectiveness Ranking

- Effectiveness   7
- Cost   5
- Core market reach   1
- Return on investment   5

OVERALL RANKING   **4.5 – C**

Yellow Pages

What do we say about the *Yellow Pages*? For years, the *Yellow Pages* has been the staple of most business advertising. With the growth of the Internet, much of the *Yellow Pages* effectiveness has been lost. And it appears that each and every day the companies, who produce the various *Yellow Pages*, particularly online *Yellow Pages*, do everything they can to make sure that the local wedding professionals receive as little publicity as possible.

The first thing I want you to do in regard to the *Yellow Pages* is to ask each and every bride you deal with when is the last time she actually looked into one. I think you'll find, that just like newspapers, most brides today do not even possess the *Yellow Pages*, let alone use it on a regular basis. This is the primary reason that most *Yellow Pages* companies are scrambling as fast as they can to promote their online versions.

When it comes to the *Yellow Pages* online, it's easy to see why it's ineffective and doesn't work. Simply go online to any one of the various *Yellow Pages* listings and type in a local service. I believe you will find that the listing you receive is virtually useless. Let me give you an example:

Let's start on Yahoo.com at the *Yahoo Yellow Pages*. I'm sure you'll find similar results no matter which *Yellow Pages* you use, but for this particular example, I went to Yahoo and then clicked on the *Yellow Pages* button.

Now let's enter "florists in Malibu, California". This is actually a very good search because Malibu is internationally recognized as a beach city in California, yet it's a very small city of just 13,000 residents. This will allow us to see how many local florists are represented by the *Yahoo Yellow Pages*. It's interesting that of the first 20 listings that come up, none are actually located in Malibu. In fact, more than 50 percent don't have a retail location in town at all. Among half of the remaining businesses listed under Malibu, the closest is in Pasadena—easily 45 miles away! After we cycle through the 120 listings of florists who can send flowers to Malibu, but are not located there, we come across two local florists who are listed.

Now, think about this: what are the chances of the Malibu bride going to the *Yahoo Yellow Pages,* entering florist, and then searching through 122 listings, only to find that the very last are actually local flower vendors who could provide them with flowers for their wedding. Now, it's true that many national companies have the ability to deliver a bouquet, but in this particular case, we're looking for wedding flowers.

Let's refine our search, and instead of searching for just "flowers", let's search for "wedding flowers". After completing a search with the same parameters as before, using the search term "wedding flowers", we arrive at a screen that asks us to select between retail and wholesale. I select retail, because most brides-to-be buy flowers retail, and that returns us to what appears to be the original listing for florists. So, you can see that if a bride in Malibu were to go to the *Yahoo Yellow Pages* and type in "wedding flowers" or, simply, "flowers", she would be given 120 options before she was given the option of using the two local florists.

It's obvious that searching the Internet *Yellow Pages* simply won't work in most local cases. If you do this exact same search in Los Angeles, you get hits for thousands of florists, and most of them won't be located anywhere near you. We also know that the vast majority of brides-to-be don't use the printed *Yellow Pages,* so, unfortunately, it appears that the *Yellow Pages* time has come and gone. Most wedding professionals can save themselves a significant amount of money by not participating in them. It appears that they tend to be grossly overpriced, hugely ineffective, and, on generating revenue for the national advertisers, the *Yellow Pages* simply represent a very poor investment for today's wedding professional.

Yellow Pages Effectiveness Ranking – Printed Book

- Effectiveness   1
- Cost   1
- Core market reach   3
- Return on investment   1

OVERALL RANKING   **1.1 – F**

Yellow Pages Effectiveness Ranking – Online

- Effectiveness   1
- Cost   1
- Core market reach   1
- Return on investment   1

OVERALL RANKING   **1 – F-**

Referrals

Many wedding-related vendors would tell me that their best business comes from referrals, which they love—because, they're free. I would agree with them. Having a prior customer refer a bride-to-be is a wonderful thing, and certainly a vote of confidence—but, I would disagree that the referrals are free.

Over the last 25 years, I had to make concessions to keep my customers happy. Sometimes, we made mistakes, and we had to correct the situation. At other times, we made absolutely no mistakes, but the customer still wasn't happy. To make those people happy, we made concessions. It's also been my experience that when we had to make concessions to keep our customers happy, it generally cost us money. Again, while we've had many happy customers over the last 25 years, there have been numerous times when it cost us money to keep them happy. So when a happy customer refers you a prospective client, you can be happy that they had the confidence and satisfaction in you that they felt they could refer you to another person, but the referral wasn't free. It cost you in the concessions you've made along the way to keep your customers happy.

Let's explore this a little further, because I know there remains a belief by some readers that referrals are the best form of advertising "because they are free". On the surface, that makes sense.

Again, referrals do in fact have a cost. Here's another way how. In order to have a bride refer you to someone, you need a happy bride. My experience has been that to keep a bride happy, the wedding professional does, at times, have to go above and beyond. Not every bride (nor her fiancé or parents) simply accepts whatever the program offers. Many times, you have to add services, reduce costs, extend an offer, or generally make concessions to keep the customer happy. In short, the price of referrals is happy customers, and the price for happy customers, more often than not, is not free. It costs you something to keep them happy.

So referrals are great. They do present you with a wonderful opportunity, but they are not free. Also, the new wedding professional who hasn't had many clients doesn't have the same opportunity for referrals as established professionals.

That's where organizations like CertifiedWeddingPros.com can help. They will provide the credibility and third-person certification that many new wedding professionals need.

Referrals Effectiveness Ranking

- Effectiveness   9
- Cost   3
- Core market reach   9
- Return on investment   9

OVERALL RANKING   **7.7 – B**

Bridal Shows

Bridal shows are a very simple concept: attract as many brides as possible by offering them an opportunity to plan their weddings in a day and to along the way see some great gowns in the fashion show. As an exhibitor in the event, your job is to do what?

With the proliferation of shows in most markets across the country, you may be scratching your head trying to decide what shows to participate in. Can an industry that applies to 1 percent of the population at any given time support 10 or 15 bridal shows a year in your market? Even if the market can support the number of shows, how do you ensure that you are going to reap a reward from your hard-earned investment?

There is also the question of what you should do at a bridal show. We have all seen the florist who arrives the day before the event and starts setting up a display. Fifteen hours and $4,000 worth of flowers later, the merchant has a beautiful booth right next to another person who walked in five minutes after the show opened, dumped some literature on the table, and started talking to the brides-to-be. Does the fact that the florist spent so much time and money on the display guarantee success? Over the years of producing bridal shows, I have seen some of the most beautiful and most expensive booths go down in flames because they did not make any sales from the show. I've also occasionally seen the person who does the least reap the best rewards. But does that mean that every wedding professional should bring a booth in a box and do as little as possible?

What about the bridal show where the promoter has promised stellar attendance, and then at the close of the show, you have met less than half the brides who were promised? You are tired; you're hungry; and you just want to bolt for the door 90 minutes before the official close of the show. You're angry that the turnout was down, and you're starting to plan your strategy to either get your money back or to receive a huge discount on the next year's show. After all, the promoter didn't deliver.

Has any of this ever happened to you? If you've been involved in the wedding business for any length of time, I'll bet that it has. And that's what this book is all about. Bridal shows can be the biggest waste of time and money you have ever experienced, OR they can be the biggest opportunity you have to grow your business. In fact, they can be both at the same time. By understanding why bridal shows sometimes don't work, we are going to provide an intelligent, organized way for every wedding professional to turn the tide and start making money from every bridal show.

Why Brides Attend Bridal Shows

Occasionally, we wonder just why a woman attends a bridal show. There are just about as many theories on why brides-to-be attend shows, as there are engaged women who attend. But I want to offer you a hypothetical situation and see if we might be able to understand a little more clearly exactly what a woman expects when she gets to a bridal show.

Now, think for a minute about a bride. She's driving down the street and hears the radio commercial for an upcoming bridal show. It doesn't take her but a second to realize that she wants to attend the show. She gets on the phone to three of her friends and invites them to attend the event with her. On the next Sunday, her friends show up at her house ready to attend the show. They all climb into the car, and just as the bride starts to back out of the parking lot, she steps on the brake, jumps out of the car, and runs back into the house. Now her friends are sitting in the car wondering what the heck is going on.

After a few minutes, the bride-to-be returns, backs out, and drives down the street. Her friends, curious to know what was going on, ask, "What was that all about?" She looks at them and explains, "We're going to the bridal show, and I knew that I was going to need my checkbook. I'm going to be writing a whole bunch of checks today, so I went back to get it." How often do you think that happens? My best guess is that it NEVER happens—for the most part.

Brides do not attend to bridal shows to purchase products.

As I said earlier, I had an opportunity to work for Las Vegas Convention Service. In fact, that's how I started in the trade show business. I worked on some of the largest shows held in Las Vegas—and we all know that Las Vegas is the convention capital of the world. It was fascinating to me to see companies spend $1 million or $2 million to set up their booth and display their products. When I first started producing bridal shows, I was a little shocked at the resistance we received from many of the wedding professionals about making a sizable investment in the events. My background and experience told me that trade shows were a successful way to do business, so I didn't understand why mom-and-pop wedding professionals, who desperately needed to book more business, didn't see the value of the show. It didn't take me long to realize that the bridal shows held throughout this country have very little resemblance to the professional trade shows being held in cities like Las Vegas.

One of the obvious differences is that in Las Vegas, the people who attend the trade shows are mostly buyers, whereas in most bridal shows, the attendees are shoppers. Now to be clear, we do know that the brides will be making a sizable investment in their wedding, and we also know that the brides have a particular idea about what they want their weddings to be. Other than that, there's little resemblance between a professional trade show buyer and an engaged woman at a bridal show.

After having produced hundreds of bridal shows over a period of 25 years, our experience tells us the brides-to-be attend the shows for the following reasons:

- To get information

- To compare prices
- To see a fashion show
- To find bargains
- To have a girl's day out and plan their wedding

My experience tells me that the primary reason women attend a bridal show is to get information. In fact, I picture the bride on this information-gathering quest. Have you ever noticed how as a bride walks down the aisle of a show, she will take any literature that is handed to her? I've often had nightmares that the merchant is standing in a booth handing out literature to each person as she walks by. Finally, one bride comes by, he puts the literature in front of her, but doesn't take his arm back in time, and the bride ends up not only grabbing the literature but his entire arm and stuffs it into her bag. I've seen brides walk out of shows with three or four bags full of information. It makes me laugh.

What are they going to do with all the literature? I picture the bride rolling around on her bed tossing literature in the air and pieces of paper flying everywhere—kind of a wedding information orgy. But seriously, what the hell is she going to do with 300 pieces of paper? We all know she's not going to read it.

At best she's going to go through the bag and throw away 95 percent of it. The rest will sit on some table some place until it gets thrown away. I always laugh when I see a bridal show promoter who has invested money in producing custom-made bags for the brides who attend the show. I think bags are a convenience that helps the brides, but there is little to no benefit to investing a ton of money in making custom bags with the show's logo on it. At best, the bag will store the literature the bride brings home until she decides to throw it all away. Promoters are better served letting a wedding professional provide a bag and using the savings to buy more advertising. And what about the poor wedding professionals who spent all that time and money at Kinko's at 3 a.m. printing the literature? Their entire presentation is reduced to an 8.5 by 11 piece of paper that's probably never going to get read.

I understand this is a fairly bleak image of what brides do at shows, but it's the truth. Brides are information addicts who attend bridal shows to get their fix. At some point in the future they may purchase wedding services, but for the most part it's not going to happen at the show.

That said, the reason you don't get the response or as much response as you want from bridal shows or your advertising is often your own fault. You are making some huge mistakes that need to be corrected.

Why Wedding Professionals Attend Bridal Shows

Over the years, I've asked thousands of wedding professionals why they participate in bridal shows, and I've had a wide range of answers. It's not uncommon for wedding professionals to say things like:

- I want to get my information out.
- I want to meet potential customers.
- I want to build rapport with as many people as possible.
- I want to see what my competitors are doing.
- I want to sell product.
- I get a list after the show.
- My competitor is there, so I need to be.

When I ask this question at a seminar, I take out a Sharpie and write the answers on a board in the front of the room. As wedding professionals yell out their answers, I always get a list similar to the one above. At some point one of the merchants will say, "To make money," which will cause all the other attendees to shake their heads in agreement. Some even applaud as if the person had just introduced a new concept that they had never considered before. I always smile and laugh a little because in my opinion, making money should be at the top of the list, not the bottom.

In truth, I believe it is at the top of most wedding professionals' lists, it's just that we live in a society where making money and surviving has been made to look like something bad. Every few days we hear about another Wall Street titan who has made $7 billion for a year of part-time work, and somehow that translates into the average mom and pop wedding professionals thinking that it's inappropriate to concentrate on turning a profit. I also believe that many wedding professionals want to make profit; they just don't want to look like a "salesman" when they do it. Profit is good, but look at this:

- Wedding professionals participate in bridal shows to make sales.
- Brides attend bridal shows to gather information.

Do you see where we're going here? The brides are attending the shows to get as much information as they can. The wedding professionals are attending bridal shows to make sales. We have two separate groups of people attending the same event for completely different reasons. A huge disconnect exists between what the brides expect to get out of the show and what the wedding professionals want out of the event.

From great challenges, come great opportunities. For now, let's clearly understand that brides-to-be do not come to bridal shows to buy product, and that is why many wedding professionals do not achieve the success they expect.

Bridal Show Effectiveness Ranking

- Effectiveness   9
- Cost   8
- Core market reach   10
- Return on investment   9

OVERALL RANKING   **9.2 – A**

Direct Mail

I once attended a seminar on direct mail, during which the speaker outlined 10 mistakes made when sending direct mail. At the end of the seminar, I had a list of 15 things I was doing wrong. When I corrected those mistakes, direct mail started working for me. One of the bonus chapters that I've added to the back of this book is all about the direct mail mistakes you can't afford to make. Without getting into specifics about how to do direct mail, let's look at it as a way to reach brides-to-be.

It's interesting that many people have written off direct mail as a way to reach brides. They assume that it's too much work or too expensive. Sometimes, I hear that direct mail isn't cost effective, and occasionally, that's correct. However, many times it's the direct mail piece that's not working, not the direct mail concept.

If you mail 1,000 pieces of quality direct mail to women on a pre-qualified list and the mail piece is designed to generate the response you want, you should receive about a 1 percent response. Believe it or not, after attending the seminar I mentioned earlier, my direct mail success rate went from 0 to 1 percent to an average of 14 percent, and it stayed at that level for quite some time. The important thing to understand is that you must have a clearly defined goal, and the goal for each type of advertising may not be the same. If you run a bakery, you would be hard pressed to expect your direct mail piece to generate 10 cake sales, but it's perfectly appropriate to anticipate 10 inquiries for information.

When e-mail first popped on the scene, there was a temporary drop in the effectiveness of direct mail, but now with spam blockers, federal laws, and the general distrust of e-mail, direct mail is making a comeback. Now, remember, the piece in your mailing has to be well done. You can't just drop a letter in the mail and expect an engaged woman to be so overcome with your written word that she wants to drive as fast as she can to your business and pay you twice for your service. Poorly designed direct mail will simply show the bride-to-be that receives it that you aren't as professional as your literature is trying to say you are. I once knew a disc jockey that insisted on placing a caricature of himself in all his advertising. What he thought was great, killed his advertising message. When he eliminated the caricature, his response rates improved.

So what does a 1 percent response look like financially? It depends on the product. If I'm selling $80 worth of cake, tops, 10 leads out of 1,000 is probably not going to be cost effective. But, if I'm a photographer, whose special wedding packages start at $2,500, it may not be so bad. In a few chapters, we are going to take an intensive look at how the numbers for each type of advertising line up, so I'll save the financial analysis until later.

Direct Mail Effectiveness Ranking

- Effectiveness   2
- Cost   5
- Core market reach   9
- Return on investment 5

OVERALL RANKING   5.1 – C

The Internet

The Internet, like many of the topics we are covering, could be a complete book in itself. In fact, you can visit any bookstore and find hundreds of books dedicated to helping you craft a web strategy. You may even be inclined to spend a significant amount of time and money crafting the perfect web page for your business. Later in this book, you will find an entire bonus section dedicated to giving you my sage internet advice, so in this chapter, I want to focus on the effect the Internet can have in building your business, not the logistics of posting a website.

In the late 1990s, many wedding professionals worried that they were going to be replaced by the Internet. Some anticipated a world where the bride-to-be eagerly sat at a computer and picked the services she needed for the wedding. They envisioned brides picking cakes, flowers, bridal gowns, formal wear, invitations, balloons, and accessories online. Then, as the wedding approached, she would take delivery of the things she ordered and cut out the brick-and-mortar wedding professionals all together. We now know that this doom and gloom scenario hasn't happened. Brides enjoy trying on gowns and seeing and touching other items. And, while a good friend of mine does sell many gowns online, it's a small fraction of the wedding dresses that are sold each year. A bride wants the interaction and assistance of a wedding professional that she cannot receive from a computer linked to the Internet.

Just as an Internet search of *Yellow Pages* online will deliver hundreds of non-local businesses to your screen, a search on the web for bridal gowns will bring you over 3,720,000 pages to view. Let's assume the average bride will be more specific and search for something like "wedding photographer in Dallas". That search yields just 4,910 pages viewing. In fact, here are some of the major wedding categories and the number of listings that come up when searched on the two largest search engines: Google and Yahoo.

Google Search by Service

- Bridal accessories – 8,790,000
- Bridal gowns – 3,760,000
- Gown preservation – 470,000
- Bridal registry – 1,140,000
- Bridal show – 8,550,000
- Bridal website – 12,400,000
- Bridal veils – 1,650,000
- Disc jockey – 8,800,000
- Formal wear – 9,270,000
- Honeymoon travel – 6,270,000
- Marriage planning – 36,900,000
- Wedding catering – 13,000,000
- Wedding chapel – 1,860,000
- Wedding entertainment – 43,600,000
- Wedding favors – 2,430,000
- Wedding flowers – 32,400,000
- Wedding jewelry – 28,000,000
- Wedding invitations – 22,100,000
- Wedding officiant – 585,000
- Wedding photo – 13,000,000
- Wedding planning – 32,500,000
- Wedding publications – 7,690,000
- Wine and spirits – 8,810,000
- Wedding video – 41,400,000

Yahoo Search by Service

- Bridal accessories – 58,200,000
- Bridal gowns – 17,700,000
- Gown preservation – 2,700,000
- Bridal registry – 13,200,000
- Bridal show – 69,900,000
- Bridal website – 47,900,000
- Bridal veils – 4,840,000
- Disc jockey – 27,200,000
- Formal wear – 41,800,000
- Honeymoon travel – 350,000,000
- Marriage planning – 89,700,000
- Wedding catering – 55,330,000
- Wedding chapel – 21,000,000
- Wedding entertainment – 273,000,000
- Wedding favors – 35,100,000
- Wedding flowers – 160,000,000
- Wedding jewelry – 183,000,000
- Wedding invitations – 49,300,000
- Wedding officiant – 8,910,000
- Wedding photo – 28,500,000
- Wedding planning – 117,000,000
- Wedding publications – 55,000,000
- Wine and spirits – 66,600,000
- Wedding video – 422,000,000

It is amazing that you can find more than 8 million web pages dedicated in some way to wedding accessories. The problem is it's just not useful to the bride. It's simply too much to comprehend.

Understanding that people would not have the ability to navigate such a massive sea of information, what did the major search companies do to ensure they were providing usable information for each search?

Nothing, except implement a bidding system that allows the businesses with the most money to make sure their listing is shown in the top few listings on every search, thereby making the search engine company billions of dollars. The fact that the search companies came up with the bidding system isn't the problem. The problem is that even though you may be the highest bidder, spending anywhere from a few cents to several dollars for each person who visits your website, the only thing search marketing is good for is bringing them to your web page. Once they arrive, there's no guarantee they will buy anything. It's very similar to the newspaper announcing that it had a new program in place where it would bill you every time someone read your ad in the newspaper. Even if they had the technology, what good would it be?

Add to this significant problem the fact that most wedding professionals have horrendously bad websites, and it's easy to see why the Internet isn't going to do much for your business. Later, we will cover some specific guidelines you need to follow to have a successful website. As I search through the web, the most egregious mistake made by 95 percent of wedding professionals is that they treat their page like their brochure—a static piece of information that outlines what they do, how they do it, and sometimes, how much. This is exactly the opposite of what works on the web. Sometime, bring up Yahoo's home page and follow it for a day. You will find the information that is offered changes constantly. Visit the page three times in eight hours, and you will see three different sets of data. If the most popular website in the universe changes data every few minutes to keep people coming back, how successful is your page going to be as a redesign of your brochure from 2001? Of course, you don't have time to update a page twice a day, but most wedding professionals don't have a noticeable update on their web page twice a year!

Recently, social networking web pages have become the rage. You can tweet or twitter all day long. I have people telling me things I never realized I needed to know:

- Mary just woke up hungry.
- Bill is excited about his day.
- Janice has a test today.
- Frank lost his German shepherd.
- Sally found a German shepherd.

...on and on... who cares? Do you care? I mean, I like my friends, and I enjoy communicating with them. But when did it become necessary to have a constant stream of information about everyone we know all the time? I understand that brides today twitter, tweet, and belch without thinking about it. So, yes, you should have a presence in Facebook, Myspace, Twitter, and the others.

The Social Networking Myth

There are some seemingly compelling statistics that backup the idea you must have a social networking campaign.

To reach 50 million users:

- Radio took 38 years.
- Television took 13 years.
- Internet took 4 years.
- iPod took 3 years.
- Facebook added 100 million users in less than 9 months.
- 1 in 8 couples married in 2008 met via social networking.
- 96 percent of Gen Y's have joined a social network.
- If Facebook was a country, it would be the fourth largest in the world.

The numbers of people who actively participate in social networking is staggering. It seems a day doesn't go by without someone asking if they can be my friend on Facebook, yet I question the effectiveness of social networking for the average wedding professional.

Assume we all go to a football stadium that holds 30,000 people sitting in the stands. One person jumps up, runs to the center of the field and says, "Everyone that likes dancing come on down and talk to me." Several people jump up and join him. Soon, other people do the same thing.

They start groups on singing, writing, weddings, and thousands more. After a while, everyone is on the stadium field participating in as many groups as they want, and the stands are empty. It's a massive talkfest, where everyone talks to everyone else. Imagine how loud it would be. 30,000 people all talking at once about every detail of their day. What would it take to cut through that noise and generate some attention?

Now multiply that by 3,333 times and imagine what having 100 million people all talking at the same time would be like. That's nearly a third of the people in the entire country, and everyone has something to say.

How can a wedding photographer in Reno, Nevada, generate sales from that? I love the thought of access to the masses. I love the fact that most of my friends are on Facebook, and I can keep them together in a group. However, for the average wedding professional trying to increase business in a short period of time, social networking is a myth.

If you're a bridal salon in Chicago, it may be good the start a Chicago Brides Without Dresses Group or join bridal groups that are in your area. But counting on a significant return from social networking without having a targeted way to cut through the noise is futile.

You should be part of the social networks. They do provide a great opportunity to share information with today's bride. However, to double your business in the next 12 months, you will need to concentrate on those advertising sources that give you the best chance to book one-on-one visits, and that's not social networking

The True Value of Social Networking

All of the social networking sites do offer a great way to checkout people who apply for jobs. When you visit Mary's Facebook page after she told you she's a quiet person who curls up with a book every night, and you see 35 pictures of her smashed out of her mind, smoking a joint topless, you may want to reconsider her application.

The Internet is a fascinating source of information that has revolutionized the world. It's revolutionized my business. In 1995, I had a 3,000-square-foot office, 12 full-time staff members, and a ton of overhead for everything from office equipment to company cars. Today, three people, spread across the world, do more work in less time than we did with 12 people in 1995. Communication is instant, because we have everything on the Internet. We don't need Microsoft Office; the program is online. We don't need servers, switches, and routers, because our database is online also. I don't even need a phone, because I have Yahoo Instant Messaging. We all know social networking will never replace the one-on-one bridal experience.

Internet Effectiveness Ranking

- Effectiveness 3
- Cost 2
- Core market reach 6
- Return on investment 2

OVERALL RANKING   3.1 – D

Social Networking Update

What a difference a year or so makes! When I originally wrote the previous section on social networking, I believed every word of what I said. I routinely debated many of the people who were running across the country screaming how great social networking was. Just as every technology evolves, so has social networking. So much so that I wanted to update this section of the book and add some information that I think is vital.

First, I want to adjust my Web Effectiveness Ranking for social networking from a D, to a strong C+, and here's why:

I've seen that in the last 18 months, you can generate interest in your product IF (and it's a big if) you promote your service effectively. Facebook has been my tool of choice as I work to expand my client base and communicate with every wedding professional that has an interest in what I have to say. By consistently working to grow my friends and attract businesses that want to "Like" me, I've been able to conduct an ongoing conversation that has lead to an increase in some elements of my business.

It takes work to insure you keep the momentum going. Every day, I post some information on my Facebook page. It may be a video or a note from a happy customer. I post anything that I believe people will find interesting without trying to sell my product every minute of every day. I've found that posting an occasional personal message about something my family is doing receives as many responses as when I post a tip for business. Obviously, I've given up a small degree of privacy, but I have been able to carry an ongoing conversation with thousands of people who would not normally have an opportunity to communicate with.

One of the advantages I have is that my products, books, CD's, and boot camps apply to all wedding professionals and if a wedding pro wants a CD set, I can ship it anywhere in the world. It may not be as easy for a wedding photographer because of the limited market area that professional has, but the principles remain the same. If you engage your public in ongoing communication that is mutually beneficial, you can achieve a limited amount of success for your business.

I've established a few simple guidelines for my social networking:

1. Limit your time on social networking sites. You can easily lose a few hours a day if you're not careful.

2. Always try to provide information that's interesting. Don't simply make every post about selling your product.

3. Respond to inquiries as quickly as possible but in your time frame. I check the page twice a day, morning and night. It's a huge distraction to keep it open on my computer and affords it a level of importance it doesn't deserve.

4. Eliminate anyone who makes me uncomfortable. I know, we live in a world where we're "good" if we are open to all and "bad" if we profile other people— well, too bad, If someone sends me a message or makes me feel uncomfortable, I simply cut them off.

5. Post video whenever possible. Youtube is the second largest search engine on the planet, and it integrates perfectly with Facebook. Post testimonials and interesting video as often as possible. People are far more likely to watch a video than read a post.

I've been fortunate that my social networking has been enjoyable, and slowly, but surely, it's becoming profitable as well. If you have an opportunity to build a base, promote your services, and have the time to do so, I suggest using Facebook as well as the many other promotional services I discuss in this book to promote your business.

Now let's rank the Internet for its ability to streamline your business.

Internet Effectiveness Ranking

- Effectiveness   8
- Cost   3
- Core market reach   8
- Return on investment   9

OVERALL RANKING   **7.0 – B**

Advertising Effectiveness Rankings Summary

Newspaper		1.2	F
Wedding Magazine		4.2	C
Radio / Television		4.5	C
Yellow Pages – Printed	1.0	F	
Yellow Pages – Online	1.2	F-	
Referrals		7.7	B
Bridal Shows		9.2	A
Direct Mail		5.1	C
Web Advertising		3.1	D
Web Helping Your Business		7.0	B

My Story – Part 3

As I sat on the dais, waiting to be introduced to the 600 people who had assembled at the Marriott Hotel in Chicago, I wasn't the least bit nervous. I knew what I was going to say. I had rehearsed it earlier in the day when the room was empty, and the teleprompter and laugh lines were all set to go. I looked out and saw my wife sitting in the crowd a few rows back. She hadn't been to a Fisher sales meeting before, but she was having a blast. Twice each year, Fisher flew all the sales representatives from all over the country into Chicago or New York for a sales meeting. These were mandatory meetings, where every sales representative, sales manager, distributorship owner, and America-side managers would attend. My job was to present updates about Fisher's training programs and to give a semiannual update on new initiatives, strategies, and policies affected by the training department.

At each meeting, a few of the Japanese managers would fly in to preside over the meeting. The Japanese managers were smart. They understood that, at that time, American managers were better-trained and equipped to sell Fisher products in the United States. Other than the occasional screaming telephone call from upstairs, we didn't hear much from them.

At sales meetings, a very lovely lady named Norico would be the master of ceremonies. She would introduce the next speaker and keep things moving. I had heard many stories about Norico and how she was related to the chairman of Sanyo. It was even rumored that she was in her position simply to spy on the American managers and report back to Japan directly. I had found her in my office on occasion, but overall, she was a wonderful lady. She would stop by my office and give me a daily Japanese lesson or tell me a story about Japan. I still have a dish she gave me for Christmas. She may have been a spy, but she certainly was the nicest spy I ever met.

Norico took the dais and introduced me. As she spoke, she said something that made me proud and wince at the same time. Had Norico knew what was going to happen within a few weeks, she would have never said, "And now it gives me great pleasure to introduce Fisher's hope for the future, Chris Evans!" Fisher's hope for the future? Everyone in management in the room understood that Norico had just signaled that I was on the fast track to upper management. In 24 months, I had already passed my two immediate supervisors in both job responsibility and income, and I was quickly approaching a six-figure income in 1982. I was 25 years old, traveling the country, staying at the finest hotels, working with retailing gods, and I was about to give it all up. I had no choice.

After I had been in Southern California for about a year, I received a telephone call. It seems someone I had met at a wedding a few years ago had kept my business card and had tracked me down. He was thinking about starting his own wedding video business and wanted to know if I would mind giving him some tips. After all, I had already started and sold a successful wedding video business.

Without flinching, I told him, "Get into a bridal show; they are simply the best way to meet brides-to-be." We talked for a few more minutes, and he said thanks and goodbye. I didn't think anything more about the call until a few weeks later when he called and asked if I knew of any good bridal shows in Southern California. At the time, Twyla Martin produced the only show I knew about—at the Anaheim Convention Center. I told him to reserve a booth at Twyla's show. I was sure he would do well.

A short time later, he called a third time and again asked if I was interested in helping him find a good show, because he couldn't find any. He had looked into Twyla's show, but she was sold out and couldn't fit him in. For some reason, that I still can't explain, I agreed to help him. Keep in mind, this was before the Internet, before desktop computers, before there was an easy way to gather the information and do market research. The best leads in the wedding business came from bridal magazines, which at that time, were in their heyday.

I'm going to shorten a very long story and cut to the bottom line. I ended up going into partnership with Frank (not his real name). Through his father, we had access to more than $100,000 in investment money. I planned to keep working at Fisher and help advise the new company. Within weeks of forming the partnership, collecting the investor's money, and having my family members and friends invest $20,000 total, we found out that Frank was a lunatic. His first "investment" from our advertising fund was to have $1,500 of work done on his car. His second "investment" was $600 in suits!

In short, Frank was an educated idiot who thought that because his instructors at USC wore expensive suits and taught him to dress for success he should do so as well. Within weeks, it was apparent that if Frank didn't have some help our first bridal show at the Disneyland Hotel wouldn't happen. Our investors would lose all their money. Frank and his dad didn't care. The $100,000 was a drop in the bucket to them and their friends, but I was worried about my friends and family who had invested $20,000. I didn't want anyone to lose money, but I knew the people I had brought into the program expected a real effort and not some sideline business exercise. They needed a return on their investment. I had no choice; I had to leave Fisher and save the bridal show business.

My first day as a bridal show producer was December 5, 1982. Our first event was scheduled for March 1983, and we had exactly 15 booths reserved, which had all been sold by my wife and a friend. We had $23,000 left in the bank and about $65,000 in commitments. In short, I started like every other show promoter— on a shoestring. The major difference between me and every other promoter was that I had a partner who had already blown $70,000. On the plus side, I had a background in trade shows from my college days in Las Vegas.

The first show had its challenges, but for the most part, it went well. The day after the show, I had a falling out with Frank. He decided he didn't want to work with me any longer and insisted on keeping the company and the $4,100 in profit we had made. His father and investors officially voted me off the board within three days of the first show.

I was out of work, out of money, and I had a house, a wife, and a 3-year-old daughter to support. A few months earlier, I was traveling the country, making great money, and working with fantastic people.

The only thing I did have going for me was I possessed the exclusive rights to do a bridal show at the Disneyland Hotel. When I signed the original paperwork with the facility, I had the license written in my name and paid for the room with my own money. I even had a written agreement stating I owned the license. There wasn't a thing Frank could do about it.

Four days after my first bridal show, I visited Gowns by Migdalia. I explained that Frank was gone. The company was now Bridal Expo Inc., and the next event would be in August at the Disneyland Hotel. She gave me a $300 deposit, and we were on our way. I stopped at a Carl's Jr. along the way to my next appointment, because it had pay phones out in front of the restaurant, and I wanted to call my wife. The booth sale was $600. Commission was $120. I told her not to worry; we could eat that week.

We managed to eat every week after that as well. In fact, over the next 20 years, Bridal Expo Inc. grew to produce a full lineup of bridal shows across the country. I've produced shows under many different names in California, Arizona, Texas, Oklahoma, and Illinois. Not all were called Bridal Expos; in fact, we stopped using that name in the early 90s. We found that as long as the show had enough advertising and publicity, you could call it anything.

Bridal Show, Wedding Show, Wedding Expo, California Wedding Expo, Texas Wedding Expo—use almost any name, and brides will come. Bill Heaton out of New York produces some very good shows called Great Bridal Expos. Bill is the master of the bridal show business. He has done what nobody has ever done by creating a quality lineup and national show tour. Unlike my first show, for which I had to cut the radio budget because Frank needed a muffler, Bill's bridal show tour has the money and history to create a quality event every time.

After 17 years of bridal shows, I received a call from my good friend Richard Markel. Richard is simply one of the nicest guys you could ever meet. Both he and his wife, Julia, have been in the bridal show business for many years, and Richard was calling to suggest I come to Sacramento and meet with some other show promoters. He wanted to form a group called Bridal Show Producers International. I missed that meeting, but I did make the next one a few months later in Atlanta. As they say, the rest is history.

To be continued..

CHAPTER 9 – Focus Your Advertising

It's important we discuss the focus of your advertising. I'm not talking about whether your advertising is elegant with a lot of fluff, or it's Spartan and very direct and to the point. That's not the type of focus I'm talking about. Those decisions are better left up to a graphic design professional who can tell you what colors attract the bride, what position on the paper each element should have, and whether you should use bold, semi-bold, or italic writing on your ad.

The focus I'm talking about could better be summarized as the core intent of your advertising. It's more a system of advertising classification. What is the core intent of your advertising, and how are you going to go about achieving the results you want?

For the purpose of this discussion, I am going to refer to advertising themes. Virtually all advertising fits within one of these themes, although occasionally some advertising will cross from one theme to another. It's important to understand these three themes, because once you know which one you are going to use for your advertising, you'll be better able to judge what the response should be and what you need to do to be successful.

The three advertising themes are:

- Informational Advertising
- Educational Advertising
- Direct Advertising

Virtually all-wedding advertising falls into one of these categories.

Informational Advertising

The best example I can give you of informational advertising would be something like the Goodyear blimp, S.T.P. Oil, or any large advertising campaign where you see the name of the product today and then purchase the product at a later date when you need it. This is also called branding.

The advertiser is counting on you to remember the product and use it when you need it. You want to build your brand recognition so strong that when people need whatever your product is, they will buy your brand. In informational marketing, the name is put out everywhere. Nike is a great example of informational marketing. How many times do you see its company logo on apparel as you go throughout your day? You may see the Nike swoosh on television, at a bus stop, in stores as you browse, and obviously, in advertising. After a time, the only thing you need to see is the Nike swoosh, and you think of Nike shoes.

Does informational marketing work? You bet it does. Every major consumer company invests a significant amount of advertising revenue into a program in which the predominant message is its logo and the company name. Informational marketing works tremendously well for many businesses, so why shouldn't the wedding professional purchase informational advertising?

What is the one thing you need more than anything else to create a successful informational marketing campaign? Money, lots of money. Informational marketing or branding promotes your company name and logo in front of the public using a wide range of advertising in the hope that people associate your brand with their needs. It takes a lot of money to do that. You need to invest in television, radio, billboards, and magazines. You need to invest in many different types of advertising so that your name becomes associated with the product.

It's been my experience that most wedding professionals have a limited budget and don't have enough money to make informational marketing work for them.

Educational Advertising

The best example I can give you of educational advertising in the wedding industry is for gown preservation. Many brides do not know it's important to take their bridal gown to a dry cleaner that specializes in bridal gowns. Some brides don't even think about it. So any company that does gown preservation needs to first educate the bride about the need for preservation, and then take the opportunity to sway the bride to use its service.

Most forms of advertising have multiple people doing the same thing. In a publication, you may have five to six garment preservation people advertising, or you may have four to five garment preservation companies at a bridal show. It becomes important for garment preservation specialists to educate the bride about the need for their services before they can explain why they're the best. Many brides don't realize they need a gown-cleaning specialist.

Wedding planning also falls into this category. Many brides start the process of planning their wedding with high hopes and big dreams about what's going to happen; they may start by cruising the Internet and looking for various services they need to create the perfect wedding. As time goes on, however, they start to realize it's taking more and more of their time each day to work on their wedding. Don't get me wrong; most brides love working on their wedding, but it soon becomes overwhelming. Then, as the wedding date looms near, and there's a mile-long list of things still needed to be done, many brides decide it's time to talk with a wedding planner.

It's important for wedding planners educate the bride about the services they perform during their initial visit and to make sure they understand the work a wedding requires. The core message for most wedding planners is educational in nature.

Does educational marketing work? Sure it does. It works very well when used properly.

Direct Advertising

Direct advertising is very simple. It means that in order to do business with the bride, you have to meet with her face to face, find out what her needs are, and create an agreement between the two of you to do business. Direct advertising creates a message saying, "Visit with me."

One other significant benefit of direct advertising is it allows you to meet every customer and build rapport. You will learn what her needs are and, most importantly, you have an opportunity to secure the initial investment. The vast majority of wedding professionals I know require some type of initial investment to hold a date or schedule a wedding. Direct advertising and face-to-face visits allow you to do that.

I believe most wedding professionals should use direct advertising. The systems and the methods you use to advertise your business should be designed to bring the bride through the door for a one-on-one visit. Few bridal merchants can deliver their services to the bride-to-be without having an opportunity to meet that woman in person. It only makes sense, that if you must meet with the bride in order to secure her order, your advertising has to motivate her to visit you one-on-one.

I've met many wedding professionals over the last 20 years who initially spent so much of their advertising message focusing on credibility or highlighting their experience that they forgot to ask the bride to visit with them face-to-face. If you're advertising theme is direct, then everything in your message should contribute to building the bride's desire to visit with you.

Find some literature you have used in the past and review it. When you read the literature, does it motivate you to take action and call your business?

What feeling do you get from your literature? There are some important guidelines to follow when creating it. These guidelines are significantly more important if your goal is to have the reader take action upon finishing the piece.

Let's take a look at some important pieces of the puzzle that must be put together to create effective literature.

CHAPTER 10 – How to Create an Effective Advertisement

Most wedding professionals have the ability to create simple, effective, advertising. As we focus on printed literature, let's review some important guidelines.

Should I Write My Own Copy?

You don't have to be a creative genius to create simple, yet effective, advertising copy. You can certainly outline on a piece of paper important features of your product that you believe are unique or interesting to the bride-to-be. Remember, your literature should have a single focus. If your goal is to have the bride call an 800 number after she reads your literature, everything you say should be designed to create that desire.

Mentioning that you have been in business 25 years or you have participated in 300 weddings is nice, but it doesn't necessarily create a desire for the bride to call you.

Offers like, "Respond by the end of the month to receive a $500 check, or call me within seven days to save $300" are generally more effective than offering a percentage of discount. There is a reason why most major retailers send literature trumpeting the savings you can enjoy by bringing a particular coupon into the store. When you visit the store, you may buy the item on sale, but you will usually also purchase additional items at regular price.

A Word of Caution

We never focus our advertising effort on price. We may offer a special to stimulate response, but if you build an entire brochure around the fact that you are the least expensive provider of a particular service, you will be cheapening your image, and you will have the business only for as long as you are the lowest-price provider. It makes much more sense to focus on the fact that unlike most wedding professionals, you will take the time to create the wedding of the bride-to-be's dreams, and then offer some financial incentive or extras if they respond. You do not need to discount your product. The truth is, I would never discount my primary service. I may add benefits and features for no additional charge, but I would not reduce my price.

I'm Not Creative.

Does that mean I should hire a professional copywriter to write my ad for me? For most wedding professionals, the answer is clearly, yes. You should hire a professional.

You can visit www.EvansSalesSolutions.com and receive complete information on booking professional copywriters, graphic design artists, and printers. We have access to hundreds of pre-screened professionals who will create your literature at a very competitive price.

If you do feel qualified to create your own literature, here are some additional guidelines regarding writing copy for your ad.

How Long Should My Copy Be?

Your ad should be as long or as short as it needs to be to create the result you desire. While there is no set formula, there are many factors that will help you determine the best copy length.

Type of product: If there's no salesperson selling directly to your customer or the item is relatively cheap, shorter copy is typically better.

What you want your ad to accomplish: If you want your ad to compel a person to act, the copy will have to be longer to convince her to do that. Advertisements aimed at enhancing your image tend to be shorter on copy.

Your product's price: The higher the price, the more copy you'll need to convince people to spend a more significant sum of money.

Where it appears: Your copy will be shorter if your ad appears in a newspaper and longer if in a magazine. Newspaper copy is designed for a short life and quick scan.

How tough is your sell: The more genuinely appealing your product or service, the less copy you will need to try to sell it. For example, if you're selling bridal gowns, you know 98 percent of all brides purchase a gown. Your copy should spend less time establishing need and more time creating the desire for them to call or visit you.

What Should My Advertising Look Like?

There truly are many opinions regarding the look and feel of every advertising piece. Some wedding professionals want bare bones, just-the-facts type of advertisement, while others believe that promoting the glamour and the dream of the wedding is important. Both opinions are valid, but remember, while a professional look is very important in your advertising, it's secondary to the response it stimulates in the reader.

If you do want to create your own literature, here are some guidelines regarding graphic design for your ad.

Use photographs.

The time for cute clip art images has come and gone. With today's computer programs and online access to thousands of images, there's no reason to not use high-resolution-quality images.

Know what you want your ad to accomplish.

Just as the copy needs to support the ultimate goal of the advertising piece, so do the graphics.

Less is more.

Remember, the goal is to have the reader read the copy, review the images, and place a telephone call to you. You do not need to incorporate 250 images of every cake you have ever made.

Understand the importance of where it appears.

Just as with copy, the graphics of your literature should be designed to fit in with the advertising medium. If your advertising is in a black-and-white newspaper, make sure your ad is grayscale and looks good in black and white. Never submit color photos to a newspaper for a black and white ad.

When in doubt, hire a professional to design and produce your advertising literature.

Free Advertising Assistance – Kind Of

We have all seen advertisements that appeal to us, and we have seen advertisements that appeal to our customers. One way of saving a significant amount of money is to look at what advertisements have worked for others and incorporating the effective parts of those efforts into your ad. It's often said, "You don't need to re-create the wheel." While it's not appropriate to blatantly copy an ad and use it (it may be a copyright infringement), it is appropriate to review ads you like and take note of what features and techniques you feel would work for you. Create a list of those features and incorporate them into your design.

The Process of Creating Your Ad

Research

You may lack experience in copywriting, but fortunately there are literally thousands of sources to learn from. Before you write or type even one word, you need to do your homework.

Immerse yourself in product literature. Gather and read all the written information from comparable companies and products that you can find. This can include newspaper articles, brochures, market research, and letters from customers, newsletters, annual reports, and catalogs.

Go through magazines and newspapers and cut out or photocopy every advertisement placed by one of your competitors. This is an especially critical step in your research stage, because you will probably get the most inspiration from this source. You don't ever want to copy or unfairly mimic a clever idea from your competition, but you need to have a precise understanding of what your competition is doing correctly and incorrectly in their advertisements.

Study television commercials, radio commercials, billboards, and print ads that capture your attention. Note especially the ones that you like and ask yourself why. Again, you don't ever want to directly copy anyone else's advertisement, but studying an ad that you find particularly creative, clever, and effective can often inspire you to create one of your own or give you an idea that will eventually spark the creative center of your copy.

Write all your ideas down. You will often find that once you begin to immerse yourself in studying product literature and existing advertisements, your own ideas will form. Keep a notebook and pen handy at all times to capture your ideas as they come into your mind. Write everything down, even if it sounds silly. Remember, it could lead to a great advertisement later on. No matter how good your memory is, don't count on remembering your good idea; always put it on paper.

Develop a Concept

Now that you know your primary product benefit and have some ideas on paper, it's time to develop your ad concept. Think of your concept and how you are going to express your product's benefit to the potential buyer so that it captures her attention and makes her want to stop and read. There are two major components to this stage of your process: the headline and the visual. If your advertisement is going to include a visual component such as a photograph, illustration, chart, or some other form of graphic, you should start to think about what it will be as you are developing your headline. Your headline and your visual are what will attract attention, and they need to reinforce one another. They should work together.

The Headline

The purpose of a headline is to attract your target customer's attention. Be dramatic, compelling, and convincing enough with a few words or a short sentence to get them to read further. Successful headlines promise to deliver something desirable to the reader. This is done in one of two ways.

Positive Approach

This type of headline tells the reader what she will save or gain by the use of your product. Here are two examples:

> ➢ "Yes. You Really Can Afford a Wedding Consultant!"

> ➢ "Our Gown Can Make You Even More Beautiful!"

Negative Approach

This type of headline tells the reader how she can avoid or reduce worry, mistakes, or wasting money by using your product.

> ➢ "Are You Ready for Your Wedding?"

> ➢ "Are You About to Pay Too Much for Flowers?"

> ➢ "Is Your Wedding Photographer a Professional?"

Regardless of whether it's positive or negative, both approaches have two important elements in common. Firstly, they instantly communicate a benefit, such as saving money and appearing attractive to others. Secondly, the benefits the headlines communicate are specific and directly related to the bride-to-be.

Many advertisements use subheads in addition to a major headline. A subhead is a secondary headline that appears either directly underneath the main headline (in smaller type) or in the middle of the copy body.

Expand on the Headline

For example, if your headline is:

"Is Your Wedding Photographer a Professional?"

The subhead might read:

"Probably" or "If He's Not a CertifiedWeddingPros.com Member, How Would You Know?"

Highlight Offers and Opportunities

Subheads are an excellent way to bring attention to your most important copy:

"Free Gift with Telephone Call'""

"Hurry. Offer Good Only Through July 1!"

The Visual Effects

There are simple yet effective options you can choose for your advertisement's visual component.

Include a photograph of the product or the benefit of using it. For example, an advertisement for wedding flowers would have a visual of bride holding beautiful flowers. An ad for a wedding coordinator could feature an image of a confused bride. If you're selling a limousine service, show a picture of the inside of the car with five happy people enjoying themselves. Many limousine companies just show an image of the car. What's exciting about that?

Use before and after images, a bridal makeup service could show a before image featuring a bride with unattractive, tangled hair and no makeup, then a photograph of the same person with beautiful makeup and hair.

But, is it OK not to have an image in your advertisement?

Absolutely! In ads where there's no graphic or visual, the headline becomes the major focus. Often, it will be larger than in an ad with a visual. There's no rule that says you must have a visual in order for your ad to sell. In fact, it would be better to forgo the visual rather than trying to use an unprofessional photograph. Concentrate on making your headline and copy as strong as it can be.

Try writing some headlines for your service:

Now, write down a subhead idea:

List any images you would incorporate:

Write Your Ad

It's time to work on the main body of your ad. The words of your body copy (the main portion of the ad) have to expand on your concept. With your headline and/or visual, you grabbed the reader's attention and introduced a theme for the rest of the advertisement. Your copy must illustrate an advantage, prove it, and then ask the reader to respond. Remember, you have to do these three things in a small amount of space. Even bigger ads aren't usually longer than one page in a magazine. When you're writing ad copy, every word counts.

First, pretend you are your potential customer and ask yourself: What can these products or services do for me and how am I going to stimulate the bride so she calls me and schedules a visit?

Your body copy should be an answer to that question. Remember, your product needs to fulfill a bride's need or desire and motivate her to action.

There are three key components to your body copy:

- Lead
- Proving statements
- Close

Your lead needs to dramatize some way your product's benefits will fulfill a bride's need. After your headline, your lead paragraph is the most important copy in your advertisement because it will determine whether or not the reader will read the entire ad. Remember, your ad needs a single focus and the lead paragraph should be written to support that focus and stimulate the reader.

Here are some ideas for writing a compelling and impressive lead and some bulleted samples to guide you:

Pose a Question and Answer It

The reader will either agree or disagree and become involved with what you're saying.

> ➤ Can the perfect wedding photography change your life? Probably not. But it can sure create great memories of your wedding.

Quote a Famous Person or Saying

This technique evokes emotion or establishes an authoritative tone.

> ➤ Time really is money. That's why you must act today!

Identify with the Reader

This will cause the reader to feel that someone understands the problems and frustrations she faces.

> ➤ You know how it is. You plan. You organize. But still, you never have enough time to plan your wedding.

Create a Fantasy

This is the most common approach for an expensive luxury item, because it appeals to everyone's desire for quality leisure time and luxury items.

> Imagine you're on a tropical island, drinking exotic drinks and watching the clear, blue, ocean waves break, enjoying the perfect honeymoon.

Establish Exclusivity

This approach makes the reader feel important.

> Because you're a CertifiedWeddingPros.com registered bride-to-be, we're going to make you a special offer.

Proving statements support your product claims with copy that supplies some sort of proof of what you're saying. Remember, brides are skeptical of advertisements, because they are paid for and generated by the seller. Brides know you're not going to say something negative about your own product. The following can be used to create your proving statements:

Testimonials

Satisfied customers can really help you create new customers. Actually, use quotes from product users about why they use or were happy that they used your product.

> "I couldn't believe it when I saw the wedding cake; it was beautiful!" – Jane Doe, Any town, USA

Endorsements

Experts and celebrities are great, because they have the power to impress people and can support the purchase of your product or service.

> Four out of five brides agree.

Awards or Recognition

> Selected as Best of the Year by a professional photographers association.

Closing Copy

This needs to strongly encourage the reader to perform an action.

The end copy is where you'll make an offer and indicate how you want the reader to respond, such as by visiting a store location or calling an 800 number. Whether two sentences or two paragraphs, your closing copy is centered on convincing a potential customer to act. Below are some specific ways you can convince the reader to take action.

Make Your Offer Appealing

If your target market is most concerned with saving money, make an offer that will save them money: $100 off or reserve now and save $100.

Limit Your Offer

Create a sense of urgency that the special offer is only good for a short period of time. Remember to keep the time frame of your offer fairly short. The longer people think they have to act, the more likely they are to delay taking action at all.

Limit the Supply

Create a sense of urgency by stating that the only the first 10 brides to schedule a visit will get something for free.

Highlight Price Changes

State that the price will be going up by a certain date. Book your 2012 wedding today and lock in 2010 pricing!

Emphasize the Gain or Loss

You should restate whatever the primary benefit is to the reader and what will be lost if she doesn't act.

Always Feature Guarantees

This is a good way to eliminate risk for the bride. Also remind her that because the product or service is guaranteed, there's no reason to wait because she can't lose.

Some things to keep in mind while you're writing:

- Focus your copy on the bride. Use the word "you."
- Construct short sentences and short paragraphs. It will make the copy read more quickly.
- Use the active voice, not the passive. For example, "You fly away to the island," instead of, "You will be flying away to the island."
- Make key benefits and product advantages stand out by bulleting or using bold type.

When you finish your body copy, read it and ask yourself the following questions:

- Does my headline reflect the strongest benefit?
- Does my lead copy have plenty of emotional appeal?
- Am I using specifics instead of generalities?
- Do I offer proof of my product claims?
- Does my copy read quickly?
- Am I clearly pointing out the advantages of my product?
- Are my sentences short?
- Are my paragraphs short?

You should answer yes to all of the above questions. If you can't, you need to rework your copy.

Some Thoughts on Design

Go back and look at ads you collected during your research. Notice the key design elements: typefaces, type size, where the text appears (columns or paragraphs), the use subheads, and the size of the headline. Note the overall look of the ad—is it fun, sophisticated, serious?

What do you want your ad to look like?

Many Fortune 500 companies spend enormous sums of money on developing ad designs because they convey the image that the company wants to be perceived. If consulting with a designer is not in your budget, keep the following information in mind as you design your own ad.

A layout is a drawing that will give you a rough idea of how your finished advertisement will look. On a piece of paper or on your computer screen, sketch the basic shape your ad will take.

If you're using a visual or graphic, decide where it will go and work the text around it. The placement of your visual often depends on how closely it is linked to the headline. If the two depend on each other to get a point across, the visual should be directly underneath or to the right of your headline. This will cause the reader's eye to flow into the visual from reading the text.

For example, if your headline was...:

"When He Runs His Fingers Through Your Hair, Do You Get Nervous?"

...then a photograph of a woman with visibly tangled hair needs to be prominently placed near the headline for the words to have full impact.

If your advertisement looks like there's too much copy, there probably is too much copy. There should be white space in your advertisement. If your copy is too crowded, chances are no one will read it. It is very common that after an ad is laid out, text will have to be cut from it.

Don't be afraid to pull unneeded information out of the ad.

Discount electronics stores do very well by featuring 25 to 50 items in their newspaper ads, but wedding professionals who are not selling their service based totally on price need to be sure to create an advertisement that pulls towards the ultimate goal of the ad.

CHAPTER 11 – Work the Numbers

Let's start this chapter by playing an imaginary game. I would like you to imagine that I've given you $1,000 that you can spend on each form of advertising listed in the following chart. Your job is to make the thousand dollars last for six months of advertising and calculate what your return would be on that thousand dollars investment.

If you take a look at the chart below, you'll see that the first form of advertising listed is *Yellow Pages*. Just to the right is the first column, which is labeled Quantity. The second column is labeled Leads/Calls, the third column Visits, and the last is Sales. The purpose of this exercise is to discover what type of response we can receive from each form of advertising.

Let's start with *Yellow Pages*. How much *Yellow Pages* advertising can you purchase with $1,000? Remember, you must make it last for six months. What size ad could you purchase in the *Yellow Pages* for roughly $150 a month or $1,000 every six months.

Most of the wedding professionals I know purchase *Yellow Pages* on an annual contract. About $2,000 a year or $1,000 every six months will typically be enough to provide you with a small, 1 x 1 inch column ad in the *Yellow Pages*. I've been told that in some areas it's much more, and in a few areas, it's slightly less. It may be different in your market, and that's fine—simply enter the numbers as you know them from your market.

In my sample, we assume the following:

- We have an ad in the *Yellow Pages* for six months.
- The ad is 1 inch x 1 column.
- We will receive 10 to 15 telephone calls each month.
- One-third will book visits – 5 total.
- We close 50 percent to 60 percent.

This is just a sample. Most wedding professionals I've worked with find these *Yellow Pages'* numbers to be very high, yet others, like flower shops, may find it to be very low. The number I want you to put in this column is what you truly believe you receive.

The next column is the most important. This is where we list how many visits we expect from the incoming telephone calls. Our experience shows us that the average wedding professional will book visits with one-third of the people who call in from the *Yellow Pages* ad. Your experience may be higher or lower, but again, we are simply trying to create a formula to measure our current position, so enter whatever number is accurate for your company.

The last column in our chart is the number of sales you capture from the visits you set. Statistically, most wedding professionals close about half of all the brides that they have an appointment with. I've had many wedding professionals claim much higher numbers, but market studies have indicated the number is on average about 50 percent. Enter whatever number represents your close rate.

Follow along with my numbers and then take a look at yours. I placed a 1-inch advertisement in the *Yellow Pages* for $1,000 over six months. I received between 60 and 90 telephone calls and was able to book between 20 and 30 one-on-one presentations. My close rate is 50 percent, so I sold between 10 and 15 weddings. In effect, my $1,000 generated 10 to 15 sales—not bad if I'm selling $2,000 photography packages, but not real good if I'm selling $85 cake toppers.

Advertising Effectiveness Chart 1

$1000 Advertising Investment Over Six Months - Complete This Form

Advertising Type	Advertising Quantity	Leads or Calls	Quantity Visit	Quantity Sales
Yellow Pages	Approx 1 Inch	60-90	20-30	10-15
Newspapers				
Wedding Magazines				
Radio / TV				
Referrals				
Direct Mail				
Web Advertising				
Bridal Shows				

The purpose of this exercise is to step through each one of the advertising methods listed and develop firm numbers for the type of response you believe you will receive from a $1,000 investment.

Complete the rest of the chart. I've included a copy of a completed chart on the next page so that you can get a sense of the general numbers we've experienced as we taught this seminar throughout the nation.

It's important to note specific instances in which there's a special exception to our rules.

Working your way down the chart to the various forms of advertising requires you to put in the number of leads for incoming telephone calls you're going to receive. The *Yellow Pages* may generate 90 phone calls; direct mail may generate 50 phone calls; newspapers may generate five phone calls—whatever the numbers may be.

In the bridal show category, however, there's a major exception. While you may only receive one booth rental with your $1,000 investment, the bridal show is the only form of advertising to provide you with the opportunity to meet your prospects face-to-face. You do not have to wait for the bride to call you on the telephone and request information. You meet her, get to shake her hand, and have an opportunity to build rapport with every prospect that comes by your booth. There is no form of advertising other than bridal shows that will provide you with the opportunity to meet hundreds of prospects face-to-face.

Take a moment now to complete the rest of the chart. Once you're done, take a look at the chart on the next page and see how your numbers match up to the national averages. Next we're going to take a look at each individual form of advertising and explore ways that you can make it work for you.

One important caveat to our discussion about advertising success is that I'm assuming that the primary goal of your advertising is to generate sales, and the way you do that is to meet with the bride-to-be face-to-face. If it's not, it should be.

Advertising Effectiveness Chart 2

$1000 Advertising Investment Ovr Six Months - National Numbers Based On Seminar Feedback				
Advertising Type	Advertising Quantity	Leads or Calls	Quantity Visit	Quantity Sales
Yellow Pages	I Inch	10	2	1
Newspapers	10 Inch x 2	15	3	2
Wedding Magazines	1/8 Page	50	15	7
Radio / TV	10 Spots	10	3	2
Referrals	?	?	?	?
Direct Mail	500 Postcards	5	2	1
Web Advertising	Varies Widely	30	10	6
Bridal Shows	1 Booth	600	30	18
			Avg 20% of Call Ins	Avg 60% Close

CHAPTER 12 – The Importance of Scheduling Visits

I hear people say things like this all the time:.

- "Sales is a numbers game."
- "Every no brings us closer to a yes."
- "You never get the sale if you don't ask."

There's no shortage of sales quotes. Interestingly enough, these quotes are not just mindless sayings that don't mean much. Sales is a numbers game; you must consistently present your product to prospects or your business will fail. In the wedding industry, for the most part, those presentations are done face-to-face.

In recent years, some wedding professionals have been trying to eliminate the face-to-face visits and let the Internet do the work for them. In my opinion, this is a big mistake. Sure, a bride-to-be may be willing to pick her songs from a song list on a DJ's website. She may even acquire a level of confidence in a particular photographer because she can look through thousands of images that person has produced, but eliminating the face-to-face opportunities that a visit offers the wedding professional just doesn't make sense for most of us. After all, the face-to-face visit works both ways.

If you eliminate the opportunity to get to know the bride-to-be, you become a faceless web page. If you eliminate the opportunity to hear her tell you how she had always envisioned her dream wedding, you miss the opportunity to explain to her how you can make the dream become a reality, and if you boil your entire closing opportunity to a series of buttons on a web page, you eliminate the possibility of explaining to the bride-to-be why she may want to invest in some of the premium features you offer that will generate greater profit. In short, you can't up-sell a bride-to-be if she's looking at a price list on a web page.

I understand that many wedding professionals cringe at the term "close" or "up-sell". I'm not one of them. I believe if you can make a bride's dreams come true and deliver the products and services she wants in a way she enjoys, it's perfectly appropriate to make as much profit as possible from the exchange. We're in the wedding business, and a business needs to make profit. The more profit, the better.

I can't stress enough the importance of face-to-face visits. In Tom Hopkins book, *How to Master the Art of Selling*, there is a great chapter about how sales champions find people to sell. Tom tells a story about a gentleman he met at one of the seminars he teaches. It seems this gentleman came to Tom and said he had the secret to sales success. Tom spoke with him a few minutes and finally the gentleman told him the secret: "See 20 people belly-to-belly every day." If you do that each and every day, you will overcome every obstacle to earning big money.

At first glance, it doesn't seem like much of a secret, but reflect on it for just a minute. Don't let the negatives creep into your brain quite yet. Let's just sit with that thought and think about how your business would be different if you had face-to-face visits with 20 qualified prospects every day. Would you make more money? Would your business grow? You bet it would. Without a doubt, you would have more disposable income, and there would be an entire list of truly good things that would happen.

In fact, there's not a downside to seeing 20 people belly-to-belly every day other than the fact that you may be a little tired in the evening. My bet is that you would be tired, but happy, because helping brides and closing sales has a way of energizing you. Many sales managers tell their reps that the best time to close a big sale is right after you close another sale. That's because there is an adrenaline rush that sales professionals receive when they capture a great sale, and right then, at that moment, is the best time to tackle the next big sale. You can be the same way. You can achieve incredible success.

I understand that 20 face-to-face visits a day would require an adjustment in your daily routine. It won't be easy to do, but then again, that's why they call it "work." You are going to need to hire some salespeople, streamline your processes, and make sure you have a solid track to run on. You're going to need a place to meet people. You're going to need a way to conduct the visit in privacy, and a solid system to follow-up and follow-through after every visit. You're also going to need a steady stream of brides-to-be so that you can schedule the visits in the first place.

At this point, I want to let you off the hook a little. Twenty visits a day is a great goal, but it's going to be very hard to achieve that goal quickly. Frankly, 20 visits a day would most likely double your business in about a month. I want to double your business in 12 months. So let's shoot for four visits every workday. It's still going to require adjustment and perseverance, but once you have the systems in place, going from four visits a day to 20 visits a day will be much easier to achieve.

It's at this point in my seminars that somebody usually raises a hand and says something like:

"Chris, even if I could fit four visits every weekday into my schedule, how am I going to get that many brides to book visits with me?"

It's simple. You ask, and you keep asking as many brides as it takes to fill your schedule.

If visiting with prospects is the key to financial success, and presenting your products to more brides everyday is the key to increased sales, increased profitability, and a better business life, doesn't it make sense that your advertising message should be targeted toward helping you book face-to-face visits?

Earlier we talked about the wedding professionals who believed their advertising should build awareness, get the message out, or generate leads for them, and we agreed that the primary goal of advertising was to generate sales. But how do we generate sales? The answer is through visiting with prospective customers.

That means your advertising should generate visits with perspective customers! In a few chapters, we are going to look at each form of advertising, and I'm going to show you how to make each work for you so that you can have more visits than you ever dreamed of.

Chris's Four Truisms

+ The amount of money I put in my checking account is directly related to the number of sales I make.

+ The amount of sales I make is directly related to the number of presentations I perform.

+ The number of presentations I perform is directly related to the number of face-to-face visits I set.

+ The number of face-to-face visits I set is a direct result of the number of times I ask a prospect to visit with me.

Do you agree with the truisms? It's important that we have this basic understanding before we move forward. If you don't understand and believe that the best way to make more money and expand your business is by presenting your product to more potential customers, then my plan won't work for you. It's possible to have other people who are qualified actually conduct the visits, and frankly, that's what you are going to have to do once you start using this system. Otherwise, you will have a significant number of brides-to-be who you simply don't follow up on. For many wedding professionals, even that would be a luxury: having so many people to get to that they can't reach them all!

To start doubling your business, we have to agree that your primary goal in business advertising has shifted from placing your advertisement with the intention of building awareness or branding yourselves to booking visits with potential customers. One hundred percent of your advertising focus is going to be that and NOTHING else. We are going to go on a quest to schedule as many visits with prospects as you can fit into your day, and when you get too busy, you are going to start training others who will do it for you.

You are no longer a wedding photographer, caterer, baker, or whatever else you do. From this point forward, you are in the business of booking one-on-one visits with qualified prospects!

Your Best Advertising Investment

Typically, every form of advertising has one thing it does better than everyone else. Radio reaches the masses quickly; direct mail has the ability to deliver a lot of information at one time; and newspapers traditionally have the most local advertising.

There is one form of advertising that is far and away your best source of one-on-one visits from brides. This advertising allows you to meet every bride-to-be in person, build rapport, and ask for an opportunity to schedule a more appropriate time to learn more about her vision for her wedding. If wedding magazines, newspapers, radio, or television could offer what this single form of advertising offers, they would charge you 20 times more than they already do. In fact, it's the only form of advertising that allows you to do more than simply wait around for the phone to ring. What is it? It's the bridal show of course!

The bridal show is the only advertising you can buy that allows you to meet prospects face-to-face. With 25 years in the bridal show business, there is a special place in my heart for these events. Please, don't misunderstand. I will be the first person to tell you that most bridal shows are a total waste of your time unless you market properly. However, the previous chart shows something very interesting.

Look back at the chart that we just created that outlines what results we can anticipate from the various forms of advertising. Did you notice that with every form of advertising, you had to first show how many calls you received and then how many visits you booked? With a bridal show, you eliminate one entire step. The fact is, the bride-to-be is standing in front of you. The bridal show easily delivers what every other form of advertising has to work hard to deliver.

I'm going to show you how to make all your advertising work for you, but first, let's discuss the bridal show. I'll bet you have participated in bridal shows in the past, and I'll bet that you have left some of those events wondering if you were going to recoup your investment. If you're like the average wedding professional, you look at a bridal show as just another form of advertising that you may do if you have the time and money. I'm going to show you how you can make bridal shows the focus of your advertising and save time and money while making all your advertising work more efficiently.

Take a moment and envision this: You have a retail cake shop, and you open your doors on a Monday morning at 11 a.m. (Yes, some wedding professionals actually work on Mondays.) For the next six hours, you have an unbelievable day. You have more than 500 brides come into your store and ask you about your cakes! Would you change your schedule that day and try to service the customers, or would you work on your accounting, take time for lunch, and chat on your cell phone? If you had more customers visit your store in one day than you normally see in a year, what would you do?

Not having a plan and not knowing how to service the customers is going to cost you tons of business. You're going to have more lost opportunities than sales opportunities, and it's going to be your fault, because you did not plan ahead. Now I know you're thinking: "Well, that's all true. However, I never have 500 brides come into my store over a six-hour period and ask for information, so this analogy is silly."

If you have participated in a bridal show, that's exactly what you've had. You're not at your store, but you certainly have a booth or a table. The brides that come to the show may not all stop by your display but most will, and you will walk away with some leads, some follow-ups, and maybe a list of who came to the show and not much more. Maybe you had a drawing and registered brides so that you can follow-up later on, but in the back of your mind, you dread making 50 phone calls to people who won't be home. Then you decide to default by sending them an e-mail or a poorly designed letter, all in the hopes of getting them to do what they have already done: stop and talk to you!

Do you see the complete futility of chasing down a bride you met at a show to ask her for a visit when you already met her face-to-face and blew your opportunity? It's not the bride-to-be's fault. It's not the bridal show promoter's fault. It's your fault.

To use a sports analogy: the game was tied, and there was no time left on the clock. You had one last foul shot to take, and if you made it, your team would go on to victory. However, you miss the shot. In fact, you weren't acting like Shaq; he at least tries to make it. He practices. You looked at the net and threw the ball the other way!

I want to be very clear. There are, from time to time, bridal shows that do not produce the results you anticipate, and there are ALWAYS bridal shows that won't live up to some of the promoters' hype. No show promoter is going to call you and say, "The economy is tough; spending is down; and we expect attendance to be off by 20 percent." It's not going to happen. However, even if you attend a show with 100 brides, you can be successful and make fists full of money, and I'm going to show you how to do it with ALL your advertising.

My experience has shown me that the average wedding professionals do little or no planning for a bridal show. If they do plan, they spend the time worrying about how they are going to decorate their booth. I'm always surprised that someone will take four hours erecting a display and not spend more than five minutes trying to decide what to do in it!

Typically, wedding professionals pay for a display as late as possible, fight for the lowest possible price, wait until the last minute to decide what they are going to do in their display, and then are SHOCKED that the show didn't go as well as they had hoped.

CHAPTER 13 – How to Make a Bridal Show Work

Let me give you an irreverent perspective from a producer of over 200 bridal shows on how to make a show successful. At times, some of these suggestions are tongue in cheek, but I have faith you will get the point.

Prepare Ahead of Time!

When you show up at the event in a bad mood because you were at Kinko's at 5 a.m. trying to make some crappy-looking flyers, it doesn't help anyone. You're not in the right frame of mind to do business. You're all stressed out, and the show doesn't start for four hours. If you simply planned a little, you could get up later, stop at Starbucks on the way, and take a deep breath. Your lack of planning shouldn't mean that everyone else has to put up with your miserable mood.

Implement a Pre-Show Mailing

A pre-show mailing is so useful and effective I can't believe that every bridal show promoter doesn't make it an automatic feature of every expo produced. Here's how a pre-show mailing works. Most bridal show producers have a list of brides that they mail to before each show. Typically, the producer will mail out discount tickets or postcards a few weeks before the event to help ensure attendance.

Contact the promoter for each show you are participating in and request he provides you the mailing list on labels 12 days before the show. Timing is important; I have found that if you receive the labels 12 days prior to the show, you can take one day to attach address labels on your mailer and then mail them 10 or 11 days before the show. You cannot receive the labels, and then mail your literature a week before the show.

Mailing your pre-show mailing piece too close to the event dramatically reduces its impact.

Your direct mail piece should highlight your booth number and make the bride an offer. "Be one of the first 100 brides to bring this card to booth #235 and receive our special Bridal Planning Notebook!" Now you have brides coming to the show and looking for you when they arrive. Be sure to focus on the mission of the piece. Obviously, you want your company name and logo on the postcard, but keep it simple. You will have time to work on scheduling a face-to-face visit at the show, so keep the copy simple and sell them on stopping at your display! One of the best postcards that I've ever seen, offered a gift for the mother of the bride for a turned in postcard. The photographer gave each bride who brought her card in a beautiful, yet inexpensive, "Mother of the Bride" pin. She also gave the bride a father of the bride present if she booked a face-to-face visit at the show. The father of the bride gift was a father-daughter photo sitting and two 8x10 enlargements. When the show closed, she had 65 visits scheduled. Just over 50 brides came for the scheduled visits, and the show generated well over $100,000 in sales.

Was it a good show or a bad show for the photographer?

You can also create the same basic program via e-mail, but be sure to use a dedicated e-mail service and only send e-mails to brides who have given the promoter permission to e-mail.

Check out www.EvansSalesSolutions.com for more detailed information about pre-show mailing programs.

Pre-Show Postcard Sample - Front

Beautiful, but plain—any bride who receives this in her mailbox is going to turn it over and read what it has to say. Postcard is four colors.

Pre-Show Postcard Sample - Back

Chris' Photography

Make Mom Happy!

Bring this card to booth #235

At the:
Big Bridal Show
Saturday, January 10, 2015

Big Convention Center
Anytown, USA - 11am to 4pm

First 100 Brides Receive A
"Mother of the Bride Gift"

Call 888-678-2008 For Details

Very simple and direct—its sole focus is to bring the card to the booth. The telephone number is for the photographer. If a bride calls for information, simply schedule a face-to-face visit.

There has been some debate about how many brides to offer a gift to. Some wedding professionals limit it to 10. I believe the more opportunities you offer, the better your chance of having a bride bring the card to you.

Have a Follow-up Plan

At every show, there are multiple types of leads that you will develop. I like to break them down as follows:

- Brides who booked visits
- Brides who said no to visits, but registered with you
- Brides who only registered
- Brides I don't want who registered
- Brides who didn't come by my display

Brides who booked visits are easy. You have a one-on-one visit scheduled within the next seven days. You have all her information, and you're done until the visit. It's important to schedule the face-to-face visit as soon as possible. When you allow more than a week to go between the scheduling of the face-to-face meeting and the actual visit, the chances of the bride-to-be not coming to see you increases dramatically. Additionally, it provides your competition with an opportunity to reach her. I've found the vast majority of wedding professionals close most of the brides they meet with, so having the visit within seven days of the show is important.

Brides who said no to scheduling a visit, but registered, are brides you have spoken to; they now know you; and they have some of your literature. Now you need to follow-up using your auto-responder system, your mail program, and at some point during the first week, one telephone call. I'll explain the auto-responder system in a bit.

Brides who only registered are a little tougher. I will place them into the auto responder-system and mail follow-up programs, but I will only call them if I have time.

Typically, this is as far down the food chain that you have to go to stay busy, but there are two more types of leads from the show.

Brides I've met at the show, but do not want to do business with, are brides who have registered at your display, but you just didn't click or who made your intuition tell you this won't work. It's OK. The brides at a show are evaluating you, and you should carefully do the same with them. We have all heard about a wedding professional who didn't want to work with a bride, and then the client turned out to be one of the most profitable customers. That's not what I'm talking about here. Sometimes, you meet people, and you have a sixth sense that this won't be good. I'm simply saying I believe you have the wisdom to make that decision, and if you find a bride or two at the show whom you feel you don't mesh with, make sure they don't get placed into your follow-up systems.

Brides who didn't come by your display or you did not meet can be contacted via the list you receive after the show. I personally believe you won't need to touch this group, but in the interest of being thorough, here is how I would work that list. First, I would cross off every bride who booked a visit, then every bride who registered at my display. This will leave you with a list of brides who came to the show, but didn't come by your display. Place these leads in your direct mail follow-up plan.

Recently, I've noticed some show promoters are giving lists that say things like, "The list is 1600 brides – 552 brides attended the show, and the rest registered for the show." To be fair, the list has 552 good leads. The remaining brides simply registered at the show web page. Focus on the brides that attended the show. Later, if you have time, you can feed the remaining 1148 into your auto-responder program, they are very cold leads at best.

Bring Great Literature

Literature comes in many different shapes and sizes. I've seen everything from the four-color catalogs that feature a high-end reception location to a black-and-white copy stuck under the windshield wiper of my car. There's simply no end to what people believe will work when they produce their literature.

I've found that once the bride-to-be leaves your display at the show, your entire presentation boils down to the literature she has in her bag and your ability to follow up. If your entire presentation is "We're the cheapest," then you can most likely use lower-end literature. However, if you're like the vast majority of wedding professionals, you want to highlight your professionalism and the quality of your work—that requires a better grade of literature.

This is another area where Evans Sales Solutions, Inc. can help. We have strategic arrangements with many national printers, and even though you can get a great price by going to many of them online, you will get a better price through my web page.

One mistake many wedding professionals make is producing expensive, high-end literature and then handing it to every bride who has five fingers. It's perfectly appropriate for you to qualify the bride before you give her expensive literature. What's the point of giving a bride who lives 50 miles away literature if she's having her wedding out of state? Chances are, she will enjoy looking at the piece, but she won't buy a thing. I understand that we are talking about a fine line, and in the overall scheme of life, a 50-cent brochure doesn't seem significant. But, handing out 300 useless brochures over four or five shows adds up to serious money.

Here's a case of EXTREME brochure control:

For years, we have worked with Ward Riggins Photography of Newport Beach. Ward is a great guy, and he services the upper echelon of Newport weddings. He always reserves two very expensive booths right by the front door of the Disneyland Hotel Show. Every bride has to pass Ward on the way in and the way out. He fills his space with images he's shot over the years, but primarily, the booth features Ward, clipboard in hand, talking to every bride-to-be. For years, this is the first thing he says to the bride:

"Hello, my name is Ward Riggins, and I own Ward Riggins Photography in Newport Beach. I specialize in working with brides who have a photography budget of over $35,000. Would that bride be you?"

If the bride passes out and Ward has to give her CPR, he knows she's not his potential client, but when the bride says, "Yes," he immediately books a visit in his Newport studio. Ward typically gets two, maybe three, weddings from a show. He's happy, and he makes as much on two or three weddings as some of the photographers make on 20.

What is Ward's secret? He qualifies the bride, and he's not afraid to take a pass when the business isn't what he wants. He's often said to me, "I would rather sit home and watch the boats than go shoot a wedding for just $10,000." We should all be so lucky.

Ward controls who gets his literature, and while you don't have to do it the way he does, it makes sense to be more than a literature rack at the show.

Have a Sales Plan and Goal

Before every show, write down a specific number of visits, contacts, and new networking partners you expect to generate from the show. Keep it realistic. Setting a goal is useless if you know it's impossible to reach when you set it. Your goal should also not be a function of need, but of efficiency. In other words, you may need 25 weddings to round out your year, but if the show is a small, midweek event with 55 brides, it's unrealistic to set a goal of 25. Two would be a more appropriate number, given that scenario. You would be able to generate two or three weddings from that event.

Share the plan with everyone who is going to work in your display. Make sure they are on the same page and have enough understanding and training to perform the job that needs to be done at the show. If any member of the team doesn't offer 100 percent assurance that they will do what it takes to help you reach your goal, find someone else. The last thing you need at the event is an uncooperative employee who's too intimidated to do what needs to be done to make the event profitable for your business.

The Auto-Responder System

An auto responder is a very cool software program that allows you to enter a series of newsletters, e-mails, or informational snippets, and then it delivers that information in whatever order and schedule you choose.

The first step is to contract with an auto-responder service and set up an account. At www.EvansSalesSolutions.com, you will find links to services that provide you with fantastic service, and you will receive a discount by registering through our site. Also on our website, you will find samples of e-mails you can duplicate to use in your e-mail campaigns.

Once your account is set up (a five-minute process), you can begin creating a series of e-mails to send to the bride after the show. It's best to keep each e-mail short and to provide some information about your company. Always close the e-mail by providing a way for the bride to link to you, call you, or register on your page. You will want to create 10 separate e-mails that will be sent to the bride after the show.

My experience shows that it's best to schedule your e-mails as follows:

- One each day for five days
- One every other day for six days
- One e-mail 15 days after the show
- One final e-mail 20 days after the show

When you meet a bride at the show, part of the registration process will be to record her e-mail address. On your registration form, you should have an opt-in box where the bride can give you permission to send her e-mails. Be sure to keep these registration forms on file in the event that there is a question later. There are specific laws that govern sending e-mails to lists. The auto-responder service you choose will provide all the information you need, and by following its guidelines, you will be in compliance with the laws.

After the show, simply enter the e-mail addresses of the brides into the system, and they will receive the e-mails you set on the schedule you created. The final e-mail in the schedule should tell the bride-to-be that it is the final message she will receive. It's amazing, but many times, that's enough to stimulate the bride-to-be to respond.

Have a Booth Giveaway

It's always good to offer the bride-to-be an incentive to register in your booth. The major advantage to promoting a giveaway is it offers you an opportunity to speak with the bride-to-be while she is filling in the form, and you have a complete list of the brides who stopped in.

Some wedding professionals wrongly believe that they should not offer an in-booth drawing because it attracts every bride-to-be who's looking for something for free, but remember, what you want out of the registration process is the contact information of the brides and a chance to ask for a one-on-one visit.

Over the years, I have seen many different types of promotional giveaways at bridal shows. Once, I had a bridal vendor at a show who offered an all-expense paid trip to Hawaii as a grand prize and a television set as a second. As circumstances would have it, another wedding professional a few booths away offered a bottle of wine every hour, on the hour, as a prize. At the end of the show, who do you think had more registrations?

The wedding professional offering the trip to Hawaii had five more registrations than the person offering a few bottles of wine. The gift you select does not have to be expensive; it simply needs to be of value. I love wine or champagne, because so many people value it as a gift.

One important note: If you are going to have three or four drawings throughout the day and you are going to need to notify winners, be sure to tell every bride who registers, "Check back by our booth on your way out of the show. We are going to post each winner's name right here." This forces the bride to stop back by your booth to see if she won. Is having the bride come by your booth just before she leaves a good thing or a bad thing? Many times, I've had wedding professionals beg me to call off the winners over the PA system. Not only does that not make sense, because you're telling one person she won and 2,000 they lost, but it makes the show sound like a K-mart store. "Attention ladies! We have a winner! Step right up to the flashing blue light."

Eat Before the Show Opens

You have something like six hours to book as many visits as you can, do you really have to take time out of the show to eat? Can't you go six hours without grabbing some putrid hot dog or nachos from the convention center concession and dragging them back to your booth? Is it really the best use of your time to sit in the back of a booth balancing some garbage on your lap, trying to open a catsup container between your teeth as you hand the bride one of the aforementioned crappy flyers? Is that really going to make the bride look at you and say, "YES, I have to have you at my wedding!"? Besides, if you paid $1500 for your booth and the show is six hours long, your 30-minute lunch cost you over $100 before you even buy the food. Eat first, but if you have some type of medical condition that requires you to graze every hour, on the hour, do it away from the booth.

Leave the Kids at Home

You knew about the show for months. Could you really not find a sitter? It's dangerous to have young children at the show during move-in and move-out, and they are going to be bored out of their minds. There's nothing a 6-year old boy loves more than sitting inside a convention hall being told to be quiet all day long. Now I realize you won't be telling him to be quiet, it's the people in the booths around you who will be doing that! Children are great. I have three, and I love them all. However, if you really need a child in your booth, simply stop every 12th bride. Statistically speaking, she should have one.

Don't Accept Solicitors

You paid to be at the show. When someone solicits you at the event to take advantage of their advertising, they are stealing from you. I believe they are only there because it's easy. They do not want to invest the time and money to research the market and reach out to potential clients the right way, they want to do it when everyone is together and someone else did the work. When you take time out of your day to discuss other advertising opportunities, you're cutting into your best advertising opportunity, the bridal show, to hear about a second- or third-rate opportunity.

The Theory of Diminishing Returns

I was taught the Theory of Diminishing Returns by Gary Brill. Gary ran a small chain of tux stores that his father started, and under his direction, they grew into a chain that covered all of Southern California.

He would routinely reserve 8 or 10 booths by the front of every bridal show. He spent a significant amount of money on a beautiful, well-lit, professionally designed display, and every staff member was trained on booking visits. Many wedding professionals would say things like, "Look at Gary's booth. That guy has so much money he can buy 10 booths!" If you spoke with Gary, he would say, "I have so much money because I buy 10 booths!"

Here's how the theory of diminishing return works:

Let's assume a wedding professional has one 10 x 10 display that required a $1500 investment, and over the length of the show, two people working in the booth speak with 25 percent of the brides and book 20 face-to-face visits. Then, after the show, they close 50 percent of the brides they visit with. Additionally, the average sale generates $500 profit. That means 20 face-to-face visits generated $5,000 profit, minus the $1500 booth investment, for $3,500 profit before staffing and literature costs. Not bad—invest $1500 and staffing; make $3,500.

Now, remember, in the sample above, two people only met 25 percent of the brides at the show. What would happen if there were two booths and the wedding merchant met 50 percent of the brides? Doesn't it make sense that they would have booked 40 face-to-face visits? They would have made $7,000 profit.

What Gary Brill did was make sure his staff would meet every bride-to-be at the show. If they met 50 percent of the brides and made $5,000, he knew meeting 100 percent of the brides meant he would make $10,000. The reason Gary's Tux Shop always did well was because Gary never left any money on the table. Like Walt Disney, he knew that the brides had "his money in their pockets," and he wanted it.

The theory of diminishing returns guarantees that if you have just one booth and enough staff to talk to half the potential customers, you would do twice as well with two booths. How many sales are you leaving behind at bridal shows because you're afraid to invest enough to make it successful?

Monitor Your Staff

If you're sending untrained, hourly employees to sit behind a table and hand out literature, DON'T. Just call the promoter right now and ask him to resell the booth. You probably won't get your money back, but at least, the booth will be profitable for someone when he sells it for a second time. I understand you can't be everywhere at all times, but frankly, you should plan on being present when your business participates in the one form of advertising that can give you the highest return.

Placing your company's future into the hands of some 16-year-old girl who's going to decide 15 minutes into the show that it's "hard" isn't going to work. She will spend the next five hours texting her friends from her cell phone, and then, when she returns to work with no set face-to-face visits, she's simply going to claim the show was bad and nobody came. I'm not trying to be hard on 16-year-old girls. I've seen employees of all ages who didn't really want to be at the show on a Saturday or Sunday purposely sabotage the success of the event. For years, we had a very successful relationship with T.J. Maxx. Its marketing manager became a good friend, and it invested heavily in our full lineup of shows. When our friend left T.J. Maxx, her replacement was appalled that he would have to work on weekends, after working all week. He didn't care that they were bringing in significant business in honeymoon wear. Within one season, he reported to his boss that the bridal shows were horrible, and they stopped participating in shows. I did miss the business, but I would have appreciated it more if he had been honest with his staff and simply said, "I don't want to do the shows. They are too much work."

As a wedding professional you must be at the shows.

Train Your Staff

It's not uncommon to have a wedding professional arrive at the show with two or three helpers in tow. In my opinion, you can't effectively have more than two people in a single booth, but I do understand that some vendors want to have more help. Three people should be the maximum you try to fit into such a small area, but however many you have, it's important to train your staff.

Quite often, the assistant a wedding professional brings is a friend or family member, not a full-time staff member. It's important to understand that the person you're bringing may want to support you, but they probably don't have the same motivation or desire that you do. That means, they don't have the same drive that you do. This shows up in the booth when they skip important steps or don't fully do the job. You may find your staff wants to slip off to the fashion show or go eat lunch together. If your staff members are young, attractive women, you may find some of the young attractive guys at the show trying to close a completely different type of sale.

My point is this: You come to the show to work, so should your staff. If you feel guilty about working family members hard, then hire someone else. From the moment the show opens until the moment it closes, you need to be talking with every bride, asking for a chance to visit, and sending them on their way. You need to train your helpers so that they do exactly the same thing. In a few pages, I'm going to give you the perfect script to use at the show. If your staff is going to book visits for you, they need to be trained on how to do it. I'm not talking about a two-minute talk given three minutes before the show opens.

This is business, not family fun time, and while the shows are fun, you need to be sure that every person who helps you in your booth has a track to run on and is committed to moving you toward your ultimate goal.

The Mary Kay Rule

Mary Kay Cosmetics is a fine company, and it has thousands of great people doing their best to be successful. Mary Kay was one of the first opportunities for mothers to join the workforce and make an income while they cared for their home. I love Mary Kay, so please accept this rule as the guideline it is meant to be and not an assault on the hard work Mary Kay representatives perform.

I noticed that it was not uncommon for a Mary Kay director to phone us and request a single booth in the bridal show. For her investment, she expected an exclusive, meaning no other Mary Kay representative would be at the event to compete. We never gave exclusives in any category, but we do offer exclusivity for companies—for example, one Mary Kay, one Jafra, one Royal Prestige, etc. It doesn't make sense to have two displays from the same company competing against each other.

Over time, we learned that the Mary Kay director would notify her subordinates that there was a bridal show and let them each pay a portion of the booth rental so they could come to the show and solicit for business. In effect, the Mary Kay director was dividing the cost of the booth between her down line, which wasn't a problem until we realized that some of the directors had down line that were 50 or 60 people long!

All morning long, we would have ladies in pink smocks showing up at the show claiming to be exhibitors. When you walked by their booth, you would see 20 people standing around. There was no way they could all fit in the booth, so they started standing in the aisle or in front of the booths of other wedding professionals. Each Mary Kay consultant would be focused on getting as many face-to-face visits as possible, but the brides felt overwhelmed, sometimes skipping the entire aisle. It didn't take long for us to implement a rule that still stands today. We call it the Mary Kay Rule. The rule is this: You cannot have more than four people in your booth at any one time, and you cannot have any more than six exhibitor badges—period.

One 10x10 display cannot effectively handle more than four people. I believe even that is too many. I would not have more than three before I rented additional space.

Plan Your Escape

The wedding professionals who start packing up their booth and getting ready to leave two hours before the show closes always amaze me. They just don't get it. While I find it's usually employees without supervision who are leaving early, sometimes, it's the key person in the business. What is the point of paying for a show and then trying to leave after only 60 percent of it? What upside is there to missing an opportunity to book more face-to-face visits?

It always goes something like this: Someone from the booth comes to the promoter and says, "I'm sorry. I have a gig that starts at 4 p.m., and we have to leave early. Do you have any carts we can use?" Now, let's take a look at the request.

"I have a gig that starts at 4 p.m." The promoter is thinking, "Good planning, the show has been scheduled for nine months, yet you couldn't think far enough ahead to cover this without making your problem, my problem."

"We have to leave early." The promoter is thinking, "We have the technology to put a man on the moon, yet you could not find a way to stay another two hours. Good planning."

"Do you have any carts we can use?" The promoter is thinking, "Sure, why not, let's flood the floor with carts. That way, brides can trip over your stuff and file a lawsuit against me on Monday. What a great idea! I get sued, and you get to be home in time to watch '60 Minutes'."

Leaving a show early makes NO sense, even if the show appears dead. Many times, I have seen the last bride to walk in the door end up booking one of the wedding services on the spot, making the vendor's day. A photographer I know in Westlake Village, California, claimed that at almost every show, he booked several visits with brides after the show closed, because everyone else was packing up and running for the door, and he wasn't. He waits 30 minutes after the show closes and then starts taking his booth down. Not only does he not have to fight crowds in the loading area, but he has 30 extra minutes at each show where he's the only photographer in the room available to talk to brides.

It's also rude to start packing your booth while others around you are trying to do business. I understand "COPS" starts at 8 p.m. on Saturday and "60 Minutes" is at 7 p.m. on Sunday. Life's rough. Let's just hang in there and schedule some visits. Anyhow, that's what DVRs are for.

As with your sales plan, you need to develop an exit strategy and share it with your staff.

Move the Table

Don't place your table on the edge of your booth and then sit behind it. Is there really a good reason to have a barrier between you and the prospect? Is it comfortable for you when you are forced to stand up and talk to people who are sitting down? Do you really need to sit down? Maybe it's time to hit the gym. It's important to build rapport and work with the brides who visit your display. You need to stand up, smile, and ask for an opportunity to meet with them!

Don't Sweat the Little Stuff

Every show promoter I have ever met strived to make the bridal show as good as it possibly could be. I've noticed that many wedding professionals get very wound-up prior to a bridal expo. They are so on edge when they arrive that sometimes I worry they are going to have a heart attack. I'm the producer of the event, and I have 300 things going on at the same time. Yet, the wedding photographer trying to unload a vehicle is about to lose it because he had to park 50 feet away from the freight door, and he can't leave his car there and block everyone else while he takes three hours to create the perfect booth.

Take a breath and don't sweat the little stuff.

If the power to your booth isn't hooked up 12 hours before the show opens, that doesn't mean the show promoter is an idiot. With the major shift to eco-awareness in most large meeting facilities, it's not uncommon for the power to be limited to 30 minutes before and after each event. I'm just guessing here, but I'll bet that even though 300 people have gone to the promoter to tell him the power is off, he can't do anything about it until 30 minutes before the show.

Take a breath and don't sweat the little stuff.

You get the point. The one thing I love about bridal shows is that they can be fun, but you have to take a breath; don't sweat the little stuff so that you can appreciate it.

Keep It Simple

Cram as much stuff into your display as possible. In fact, be sure to rent a U-Haul, fill it with everything from your 1,500-square-foot store or office, and try to re-create it in the 100-square-foot space you rented at the show. Brides love it when they come to your display and have no idea what you do. Just because it looks like a thrift store doesn't mean they won't stop.

I'm just kidding here. Years ago, I taught an entire seminar on how to design a booth for a bridal show. I presented it many times. It was a four-hour seminar that basically came down to this: The bride must recognize what you do when she looks at your booth. If she doesn't know what you do within 5 seconds, your design is wrong. If I were designing a booth today, I would bring nine things in one box that I could easily carry in one trip.

1. A properly sized, professionally produced banner that clearly shows what I do(with six sign hooks)
2. A scheduling book
3. Confirmation receipts – two part
4. 1,000, four color, professionally produced brochures
5. Two pens (one is a back-up)
6. Two bottles of decent wine (Ciello Merlot would be good)
7. Wine drawing entry forms
8. Three bottles of Fiji water and 3 VPX Protein Bars
9. Nu-Breath breath mints

I would dress conservatively and enter the convention hall 90 minutes prior to the show. I would carry my one box to my booth, hang my banner, and start working. With 85 minutes left before the show opens I would start meeting other wedding professionals I don't know (who weren't busy) and start booking face-to-face visits so that we could start networking. I would say hello to those I did know, but spend time with the ones I haven't met before. With 15 minutes to show time, I would put the rest of the items from my box on the table in the back of the booth, go to the bathroom, eat an energy bar, drink some water, pop a breath mint, and be ready ask each and every bride-to-be for an opportunity to visit with her and discover her vision for her wedding.

The reason I would make it all fit into one box that I could carry in one trip is because occasionally you will participate in an event at a union facility. The union charges for move-in and move-out at a union facility, and while $900 to have one person pull a cart full of literature seems appropriate to the union, it seems like legalized robbery to me. You can always carry one box and not violate the rules.

I truly believe that one or two people, intent upon booking face-to-face visits, can work from a display space with nothing more than the list I gave. You do not need $5,000 in flowers or 15 photography books. It seems that most DJs believe that the bride hasn't heard their message until they see them walking away from their booth with their ears bleeding. If I were a DJ, I would leave the equipment at home and concentrate on booking face-to-face visits.

How to Book Face-to-Face Visits at the Show

Follow my guidelines word for word for booking visits. Do not change anything other than the place where your name and business fit in. (It would be silly for you to use my name.)

Here's the phrase that is going to change your life:

Hello, my name is Chris. I own Chris's Flowers. We specialize in one-on-one attention with every bride we work with. In order to do that we need to, let's sit down and talk so that you can tell me about your dream wedding. Obviously, we can't do that here at the show, so when would be the best time to schedule a visit so we can talk about your wedding: mornings or afternoons?

That's it. Some important points to remember:

- Smile, and look them in the eyes.
- Don't change anything but the name and business.
- Don't stop after, "Here at the show," it's not a period. It's purposely a run-on sentence.

- Don't stop after "your wedding."
- Be prepared for the bride-to-be to say, "What?"
- Repeat, word for word.

You can change the name, position, and company name but nothing else. Many times, I've seen businesses hire sales professionals and then give them a script to use as they learned the sales process. Many times, the sales manager will say, "Here's the script we use, try to stick with it as much as possible." Then the new reps look over the script and make a few small changes, because they want to be "comfortable" as they go through it.

In sales, being comfortable is very overrated. Many times, when your sales reps are comfortable, that's just a nice way of saying ineffective. Companies spend thousands of dollars to have people write incredibly effective scripts that work extremely well, and then let the sales rep with no experience change the script to be comfortable.

I don't care if you're comfortable. Use the script word-for-word, and when the bride-to-be gives you the doe-eyed "what?" look, simply repeat it. When people say "what," it doesn't mean they didn't hear you. Typically, they are trying to formulate a response and need some time—we all do it. Simply say the same thing again.

Don't Sell Your Product at the Show

I'm assuming your product falls in the major wedding categories. If you're at the show to sell wedding gown-shaped potholders, then skip this section. If you're anyone else, read on.

At a bridal show, you are going to have just a few minutes to meet the bride-to-be, ask her to enter your in booth drawing, talk to her, and request an opportunity to visit face-to-face. It happens very quickly.

Let's assume you are a wedding photographer and a bride comes to you and starts asking 150 questions—questions like the following:

- What packages do you offer?

- How much does it cost?
- Can my brother shoot some pictures to save money?
- What type of cameras do you have?
- How do you dress?
- Can I pay you after the wedding?
- Can I get the negatives for free?

It's happened to you, so I know you can visualize the bride I'm speaking about. She has tons of questions and simply wants to hang out in your booth and talk for hours on end.

Maybe it's not an inquisitive bride. Maybe it's a bride and groom, and they seem like they are ready to select their photographer. They simply want to review the images you have in your books, talk about the price, and then start working with you to make a short list for the wedding. They have money, and all they need is about 60 minutes of your time. You know you can get the deposit. Do you do it?

Many photographers would, and in my opinion, they would be making a mistake. You see, I don't think in this case a bird in the hand is worth two in the bush. By taking 60 minutes to book one sale, you are going to miss far too many sales to make it profitable.

Have you noticed that when an exhibitor at the show is busy, all the brides simply wait in line until the wedding professional has time to talk to them? Neither have I. If you don't greet the bride and start talking to her within three seconds, she's gone on to the next display. Why would you miss 20 percent of the brides at a show in order to book one wedding?

There is an easy solution, and it's simply this:

"You know, I am excited as I can be to work with you on your wedding, and I know you have a ton of questions. I want to answer all of them, because we specialize in one-on-one attention with every bride we work with. In order to do that, we need to sit down and talk so you can tell me about your dream wedding. Obviously, we can't do that here at the show, so when would be the best time to schedule a visit so we can talk about your wedding: mornings or afternoons?

Network for Dollars

I once had a gentleman working for me named Steve. Steve was a great salesman. We actually hired him out of a tux shop in Tustin, California. As a tux shop manager, he knew about talking to the clients, but he had never gone out and called on clients face-to-face. As it turned out, he excelled at it. In a very short time, he had an extensive network of friends and clients that he worked with regularly. He absorbed our sales system and became a champion salesman.

After several years, he decided he wanted to take on other challenges, and he left our company to go to work as the marketing vice president for a major carpet manufacturer. One of his responsibilities was to attend an annual trade show in Las Vegas and supervise the sales team the company brought in to work the show. His company invested hundreds of thousands of dollars in the show, so it needed a return.

At the show, he quickly noticed the majority of sales reps were meeting with existing customers and showing them the new products. Typically, the presentation would take quite some time, because the client and rep knew each other. Thus, they discussed much more than just carpet. The reps would meet a client for breakfast and then work the trade-show floor for a couple hours. Then they would meet a client for lunch.

After lunch, they would come back to the trade-show floor for a few hours and then run off to take a client to dinner. This had been the routine at the carpet show for many years. There were plenty of representatives at the show; they were just all busy talking to clients and friends.

The next year, he introduced a new system. He explained to the sales reps that they should call their existing clients before the show and set-up one-on-one presentations to highlight the new products, but they were to have the appointments within seven working days after the show. At the trade show, they could say hello to existing clients and spend a few minutes visiting, but they were not going to do presentations at the show for existing clients. Also, there wouldn't be any client breakfast, lunch, or dinners at the trade show. The reps were to be on the trade-show floor as much as possible during show hours. If they did take someone to lunch or dinner it had to be a new client or prospect whom they did not have an account with.

At first, the sales reps were in an uproar. They thought he had lost his mind. They tried to convince him that existing customers would be outraged if they couldn't go to dinner, and they would feel snubbed. Each rep tried his best to plead his case for why he had to go party with his clients at company expense until 2 a.m. Of course, quite the opposite was true.

The clients loved the fact that they received a one-on-one presentation in their store. The company extended the show prices, and it actually received more orders than it typically did at the show. The benefit to the carpet mill was that it had a fully staffed booth every time a new prospect came to the display. It opened 88 new accounts at the show. In prior years, it was lucky to have opened 10.

The company lowered cost, took care of the customer, and expanded its sales base all because Steve refocused the sales team from having a three-day party in Las Vegas to working. He was a hero and actually moved up the corporate ladder very quickly. He's now the vice president of the entire company.

How does this apply to the wedding professional? At every bridal show, you will have an opportunity to meet and network with other wedding professionals. I have noticed that many of them who have done shows for years have a tendency to seek out the other professionals they know and then stand around and talk to them. The point of networking at the show is to build new relationships and expand the relationships you already have. In a 150-booth bridal show, there are about 140 opportunities for you to get referrals.

Take time before every show to walk the floor. Don't do it during the show, you will miss brides. Don't spend more than a minute or two with each professional. If I'm a wedding photographer and I see the owner of a flower shop, I'm going to say this:

"Hi, I'm Chris with Chris's Photography. I love your display. You know, I occasionally have brides who ask me about flowers, and I'll bet you sometimes have a bride ask about photography. I know we can't do it today, because we're both busy, but I was wondering when would be the best time to visit with you and see how we could start referring business to each other. I'm thinking we could meet at a Starbucks. Would it be better to meet in the morning or afternoon?"

See how simple that is? You don't need to discuss the weather, sports, or how bad the economy is with some other wedding professional you have known for years. Schedule face-to-face visits with the other professionals and start networking business with each other.

When's the last time you walked out of a bridal show with 35 bridal and 15 merchant visits scheduled?

CHAPTER 14 – How Many No's Will You Get?

Here's the question:

If you ask 100 percent of the brides at a bridal show for an opportunity to visit, how many will say no?

I understand that many wedding professionals believe that not all brides visit all the displays at a show, and while I agree with the premise, I disagree with the percentage usually quoted. When a bride-to-be attends a bridal show, it's generally believed that she does so with two other people. If you use Southern California as an example, that means the bride travels an average of 15 miles and pays somewhere between $8 and $10 for parking. Then she invests between $8 and $15 per person to attend the show, meaning the average woman has an investment of between $32 and $55 to attend a bridal show. How many brides invest $32 and then skip a large percentage of the displays? I don't believe many do.

However, that doesn't mean that every wedding professional sees every bride. As discussed earlier, an exhibitor whose display is closed off and uninviting is going to meet far fewer brides than a wedding professional who has an open display, great attitude, and is standing ready to meet people.

For our discussion here, I'm going to assume you have a great booth, fantastic attitude, and you are ready to meet and talk with every bride-to-be who walks by your display. When all those things happen, I know for an indisputable fact that 95 percent of the brides who attend the show will walk by your booth. But just for the sake of discussion, let's assume I'm wrong, and only 80 percent of the brides come by your booth—and you speak with only 80 percent of them.

Here's our show example:

- 1,000 brides attend a bridal show.
- 800 brides walk by your display.
- 640 brides stop in your display.
- If 640 brides stopped by your display and you used the script I provided word for word, how many brides would say that no, they don't want to visit?

While you're thinking about that, let's discuss these numbers a little more. Can you talk to 640 brides in one day at a show? While I understand that every show is different, I think it's safe to assume most shows are open to brides from 11 a.m. to 4 p.m. Some open earlier, some close later, but a conservative time frame is five hours to meet brides. Take 640 brides divided by five hours, and that means an average of 128 brides per hour (if they were spread evenly). If you have two people in your booth, you each need to talk to 64 brides per hour. Even using my script and being efficient, it's not realistic to assume two people could achieve that level of success. So you either need to hire and train one more person to work the show or you're going to miss speaking with some brides. My experience has shown that 45 brides per hour is about the best one person can perform at a bridal show and still be effective.

If we divide our 128 brides per hour by three, we have 43 brides per hour each. This is well within the optimal range. We don't have an extended period to talk to the bride-to-be. but we can present our script and ask for an opportunity to visit. Knowing that you can adequately service 640 brides at a show, let's return to the question.

"No" Your Way to Success

If 640 brides stopped by your display and you used the script I provided word for word, how many brides would say that no, they don't want a face-to-face visit?

Here are your choices:

- 10%
- 25%
- 50%
- 70%
- 80%
- 95%
- 100%

How many brides will say they do not want to visit you?

Our experience tells us that when you first start focusing on scheduling face-to-face visits at the bridal shows, 95 percent of the brides will refuse to book a visit. That's the bad news; the good news is that 5 percent will say YES! Over time, your average will increase, and I know many wedding professionals who average an 8 to 10 percent success rate.

When is the last time you walked out of a bridal show with 32 face-to-face visits scheduled? I'm going to show you how to ensure the vast majority of those brides actually show up for the visit in a minute, but think about that for one minute. You have 32 opportunities to visit face-to-face with a bride and tell her your story. In my experience, most wedding professionals do very well with face-to-face sales opportunities.

Even if we assume that 20 percent of the brides will not keep their scheduled appointment that leaves 25 brides who you do see. Having met thousands of wedding professionals over the years, I know a closing ratio of 50 to 80 percent is not uncommon. That should translate into between 12 and 20 sales, and that's before you do any follow-up!

When is the last time any newspaper, wedding magazine, radio commercial, or direct mail brought you 12 to 15 sales? Remember, these are sales that should all happen within a week of the show because the smart wedding professional NEVER books face-to-face visits at the show for more than a week away. You must strike while the fire is hot!

I understand that many of these numbers are estimates, but they are based on years of experience. Let's assume the show only has 300 brides. That's a little disappointing, but at least you will have time to talk to every bride. Five percent of 300 is 15 scheduled visits.

Three of them most likely won't show up, and you will meet with 12. That translates to between 6 and 9 sales. Is that a good show or a bad show? And remember, you haven't even begun to follow-up on the 95 percent of the brides who wouldn't meet with you!

Let me ask you this:

If you ask 100 brides for an opportunity to visit with them and 100 percent say no, how many face-to-face visits do you have?

Now, don't ask any brides to meet you, and many visits will you have?

It's the same—zero. When you attend a bridal show and don't ask for appointments, you are wasting the vast majority of your investment and you are not being as professional as you should be. It's interesting that a wedding photographer would never leave an expensive lens out in the rain, because he would be losing quite a bit of money, yet that same photographer will invest in a wedding show and then completely throw his money away by not working effectively.

Helpful Friends

You are standing at your display, and the show just opened. You forgot to tell your friend who's helping you about asking for appointments, so at the last minute, you tell her something like this:

"Oh, I forgot to tell you. I just read this book, and it explains that the best thing to do at a bridal show is to schedule appointments with brides. They don't call them appointments; they call them visits. What we need to do today is schedule as many visits as we can." Your friend looks at you like you are from Mars and says, "How are we going to do that?"

Not wanting to be rude, you say something like, "Don't worry about it. I'll do the first 20 brides, and you can do what I do." Your friend is happy, and you think you're back on track.

The first bride comes to your display. You take a deep breath and give her the presentation, to which she says, "No thanks, I'm just looking around. I don't want to meet with anyone yet." You think, "That wasn't hard, but I didn't schedule a face-to-face visit."

Bride two comes up; she says no. Brides 4, 5, 6, 7, 8, 9, 10, 11, 12, 13, 14, 15, 16, 17, 18, and 19 all say, "No, I don't want a visit." Brides 20 to 50 say no, and so do brides 51 to 80.

At this point, your friend looks at you and says, "You have some type of system? Was the author of the book from California? They're all nuts, you know." And because you're discouraged and slightly embarrassed, you smile, stick out your arm, and start dropping literature into the bride's bags as they walk on by, gathering literature for the informational orgy that's soon to follow.

This is HARD! You need to work the show to make sales, and this is just about as hard as it gets. While the other vendors are eating, watching the fashion show, and visiting with their friends, you're in your booth having 95 percent of the brides reject you to your face!

But, at the end of the day, when everyone is packing up and the person next to you says, "I don't know. I think I saw three brides who will be calling me for sure," you're going to have to bite your tongue not to scream out, "I have 35 face-to-face visits! Thirty-five brides are coming to see me this week! I love this show!"

My daughter participated in a bridal show earlier this year. A few years ago, she decided that she wanted to help brides coordinate their weddings, and frankly, she's very good at it. She's developing a very good client base of affluent Malibu residents, and things are going well. She attended the show to see how many face-to-face visits she could set, but she also wanted to be selective and qualify brides before she agreed to visit with them. The show was sold out, but the promoter offered her a half booth space that she could share with an officiant.

At the show, she started by using my script, and then, once a bride expressed interest in getting together, she would qualify them a bit more before firming up a specific time to visit. After a few hours, her booth partner said, "I can't believe how many people you're meeting with, and that's only about half of the people you could have met with. Please, teach me what you are doing."

She gave him a five-minute training seminar, and with no script and no experience, he managed to book four face-to-face visits in the last few hours of the show! He was thrilled and said the show was already the best show he had ever participated in. On his way out, he renewed his space for the next show.

I told my daughter when she relayed this story that she should have received a commission from the sale. After all, it was her training that made it possible for the officiant to do so well. Remember, the script isn't hard and talking to brides isn't hard. **It's sticking with the system when everyone else is doing something different that's hard.**

Guidelines for Getting No's

- Talk to every bride.
- Repeat the script for every bride.
- Train anyone who is helping you prior to the show.
- Train in front of a mirror.
- Test each other.
- Don't give up!

Nail Down the Face-to-Face Visit

With only 5 percent of the brides agreeing to set a face-to-face visit, I think you will agree that it's important to have as many of the brides as possible show up for the visit, isn't it?

On technique you can use to ensure a higher degree of commitment from the bride is a very simple process designed to do nothing more than establish, in the bride's mind, that you are already doing some type of business together. When you finish a transaction at any store, from 7-Eleven to the grocery store, what is the one thing they always give you? A receipt, of course. And if you ever need to follow-up with a store you have done business with, the first thing you'll be asked for is the receipt. Psychologically, the receipt indicates that we are doing business with the other party.

At the show, when a bride schedules a face-to-face visit, have a two-part form. On the form, have a place for all the bride's contact information as well as a place to write in her visit time, date, and a place to OK the paperwork. If you have specific directions to find your location, then place a map on this form as well.

When the bride-to-be agrees to come by on Thursday at 11 a.m., simply enter all the information, hand her the slip, and ask her to OK it with her signature. Rip off her copy and hand it to her. This step is designed to do nothing more than cement into the bride's mind that you have a scheduled face-to-face visit and the time and date of that visit.

It's the next thing you are going to do that will be the most powerful.

Visit Reminder Sample Form

Visit Reminder

Name _____

Address _____

City _____ State _____ Zip _____

Cell _____

Work _____

Email Address _____

I will add you to my email list and send a reminder.

We are scheduled to visit together

Date _____

Time: _____

Location: _____

Signature: _____

Bring as much information as you want. I'm excited about having a
chance to start planning the wedding of your dreams.

_____

Qualify the Bride

At this point in the process, the bride thinks she's done, and she's
ready to go on to the next display. But, as sales professionals, there
is one more step we have to take to provide ourselves with the best
opportunity of closing the sale when we meet with her. This step is
very powerful, and you should do this with every face-to-face
presentation you set up.

Just as the bride is turning to leave, you say:

"Oh, Diane, one last question. Is your fiancé, John, or your mother going to be helping you pick your flower arrangements?"

She's either going to say, "Well, yes, John is intimately involved in every aspect of the wedding. In fact, he's over at the equipment rental booth this very minute selecting the fabrics we will be using to cover the chairs." Or, "John is only interested in one part of the wedding, the honeymoon. I'm doing everything." Either way, it doesn't matter. It's just the information you need. If the bride says she's the sole decision maker, then say goodbye and send her on her way. However, if she says someone else is going to help her with her decision, it's important to make sure she brings that person to the face-to-face visit. If she doesn't, you are setting yourself up for the, "Let me check with John and get back to you" objection.

Here's how you handle it if she says her mother will be helping her. You say:

"That's great. Is she going to be able to be at the visit with us on Thursday, or should we reschedule for a time when she can be there?"

It's clean, simple, and tells the bride that you want both decision makers there without being pushy.

Occasionally, wedding professionals in my workshops have said, "Isn't that a little strong?" I have to smile, because if qualifying the bride is too "strong" for them, then what they are about to learn at the workshop and what you are about to learn in this book will make them pass out. Let's just say that I've never heard of a bride who cancelled the appointment and ran off because a wedding professional asked if all the decision makers were going to be there. Again, you should do it word for word. It's easy, and it works.

Does this mean that Diane will always show up or show up with everyone you need to close the sale? No, but by qualifying the bride-to-be just a bit before the actual presentation, you will be laying the groundwork for closing success, and that's what is going to help you double your business, closing every sale opportunity.

E.S.S. Text

Many times people as me what's the best suggestion in my book. Until I had an opportunity to add this updated section in the first revision, I always had to search for any area of the book I felt was stronger than others but now it's clear. If you don't learn or are not motivated by any section other than this, your business will improve.

ESSText is a texting service that started under the name of Text-Me-Now. I discovered the service and started using it for my own marketing. Once I saw the unbelievable power of this text program I began recommending it to my friends and clients. Of course they all wanted to know what the name of the program was and I truthfully didn't have a name. We created the Text-Me-Now name because we thought it explained what the program does. It wasn't long before a couple hundred of my largest clients were using Text-Me-Now.

Within a short time, we began to see problems with the implementation part of the texting program. It wasn't uncommon for the service to be down for four or five days. We would contact the service provider and receive a message or a text that said, "It will be fixed tomorrow." With two hundred people using a program that I recommended, you can imagine the telephone calls and emails I was receiving! After a couple months of ongoing issues wit the service provider (not the service) we made a decision. We contacted the service provider and bought them out. We now own all the rights to a very cool texting service but to be clear that the service had changed we renamed it to E.S.S. Text, for Evans Sales Solutions Text. ESSText is simply a fantastic implementation of technology the brides are in love with already.

I want you to visit your local mall and watch women as they walk up and down the mall shopping. Now I'm not talking about doing a creepy way for people to look at you and wonder what you're doing but I want you to do some research to truly understand the huge potential that in front of you right now. I'm confident that when you go to the mall and watch people walk by, you'll see that about 90% of all women have a brand-new appendage.

That appendage is the newest smart phone they can possibly purchase. In fact it's not uncommon to walk to the mall and almost bump into people because they're not just walking anymore. People don't simply go to the mall and shop. They shop and text at the same time. Text is the latest revolution in technology and its really snuck up on us.

A few months ago AT&T announced that they now handled more text messages on their network than telephone calls. Think about that for a second, the telephone has been around for a hundred years. Cell phones have been around for 20 plus years and now within just a few short years texting between people has become more popular with much of the population than telephone each other.

I must admit, I was a little in denial when I first heard about texting. It may be because of my age but I couldn't figure out why someone would text a message rather than just call on the phone but what I've learned is that while it may seem counter intuitive to text people rather than call text thing is quicker, easier and gets more done faster than telephoning someone.

I recently had an experience where my 14-year-old daughter was sitting in the back of the car with her friend. We traveled quite a ways and both of them were sitting and they weren't saying a word. I thought it was a little bit strange that they were silent so I said to them, "Don't you guys talk anymore?" my daughter quickly replied, "We are talking." I took a quick glance and realized that both of them were sitting there in the car texting each other. It's interesting that for them it was perfectly appropriate to sit next to each other and text. Now, some of the people I've told the story to think they've would be texting because they didn't want me to know what they were saying, but I think it's a lot simpler than that. I think they text each other all day long, that's what they're used to. Texting is as natural for them as calling on the phone is for us.

As you deal with brides you have to understand that there's a new dynamic in their life. In the 40s people hurried home at night to listen to the radio. In the 60s people came home at night and watched TV. That continued for the most part right up until the Internet was born. The minute our friend Al Gore finished the Internet a new dynamic came into all of our lives and things were never the same. Now we can't live without the Internet.

Then came cell phones and yet again technology was revolutionized and the world changed. Now we're at a point where smart phones like the Apple iPhone and the Droid, and all the other phones that are being introduced provide a new dynamic.

Technology and our world has dramatically changed yet again. We must reach out to brides using the technology that they understand. Just as the Yellow Pages in the printed form is virtually dead, text is the latest technology that every one's excited about. Recent studies have shown that even e-mail use is starting to decline because there are new technologies that people would rather use. The new technology is texting.

As I teach my Bridal Business Boot Camps across the country I ask people what they know about texting each other. It's interesting, there's a very clear line of distinction between those individuals who appear to be over 40 years old, and those who appear to be younger than 40. The younger generations certainly understand the importance of texting and they use it on a regular basis. That's why it's very important for you as a wedding professional to make sure you stake out your territory and use texting as a way to generate business.

I want to be clear, I'm not talking about the type of text program where you sit on your phone and sent text to brides who may be interested in your product. Certainly that's an option that's available under the program we've developed but more importantly the program we've developed is designed so you, as a wedding professional, can reach out and put information in the brides hands instantly whenever she requests it.

Imagine this, a bride is sitting at home thumbing through a bridal magazine at 11 p.m. She sees an ad that interests her and she wants more information. Many recent studies have shown that she is very unlikely to get up, go to her computer and search out the vendor highlighted in the advertising. If the ad has an option to text for information she is very likely to pick up the smart phone she's already used that day to text an average of 85 times and use it to request information. You as a wedding professional have the opportunity to put information in the bride's hands at exactly the moment she wants it.

ESSText allows you to secure a keyword. Let's say I have a formal wear store name Chris's Tux and I aquire the key word ChrisTux. In all my advertising I place a small line that says, "TXT ChrisTux to 59925".

Brides who see the ad know that if they text the word, ChrisTux to 59925 they will receive information. When they do text you, they provide you the perfect opportunity to give the bride information about your product or service and provide her with a link to your webpage. You can also capture the bride's phone number and build a database of brides have requested information from you. This can be very valuable later when you're ready to run your big weekend special and you have a list of three or 400 brides who have registered on your text page. You can send them a text that says, "Don't miss the big sale this weekend at Chris's tux."

I don't want you to think of text in the bride is something where you have to get on your computer and send a message to 300 brides. Instead understand that over time as more and more brides register and you capture more and more information you will be building a database of brides who have not only been interested in your product, but who have been led by your primary message to your website so they have some education about you. The beauty of this new technology is that you're putting information in the bride's hands exactly when **she requests it.**

Just as it would be foolish not to have a webpage, I believe at this point in time it's foolish not to protect yourself and own your own keyword for texting.

As with any Technology, this information changes on a regular basis so it's important that you visit my web page for updates. Go to:

www.EvansSalesSolutions.com and click on Resources, or simply text ESSText to 59925 for a sample.

CHAPTER 15 - The Perfect Presentation

Here we are, the moment we have been working for, the moment when we visit with the bride face-to-face and receive her order. This is your opportunity to learn about the bride-to-be and what her dream for her wedding is. You can find out what her needs are and start formulating a plan to fill those needs.

Most wedding professionals understand the need to take time with the bride-to-be to find out what she wants. We have all heard the saying, "God gave us one mouth and two ears so that we could listen twice as much as we talk." We've all heard it; most try to abide by it. In recent years, it's become fashionable to talk about the presentation being an educational opportunity, and various speakers are touring the country giving seminars about the need to "educate" the bride and then close her. I certainly don't want to take away from their good work, but my experience has been that some brides are just too hard to educate! I want to close them, not send them to college.

To that end, I've always believed, "A smart man knows his limitations." Keeping that in mind, I once again want to remind you about what I believe is the best overall sales training book you can invest in. *How to Master the Art of Selling* by Tom Hopkins has page after page of information about conducting the perfect presentation. You can get a copy of the book by visiting www.EvansSalesSolutions.com.

I do have a formula that I like to use when I'm conducting a presentation. It's simply a process I have developed that allows me to present my information in an orderly way and that leads me to the best possible opportunity to close the sales. First, let me ask you a question:

What Is the Primary Purpose of the Presentation?

If you are like most of the wedding professionals who attend my seminars, you will answer like this

- To Tell about your product
- To learn about what the bride wants
- To explain features of your service
- To find out the bride's budget
- To build a relationship with the bride
- To answer her questions

It's true that all of the things listed above are important, but they are not the purpose of the presentation. They are simply a part of the presentation. The presentation offers you an opportunity to tell the bride about your product, but that's not the purpose of the presentation.

Think of it this way. You are not meeting with the bride to:

- Tell her about your product
- Learn what she wants
- Explain features of your service
- Find her budget
- Build a relationship
- Answer questions

Why are you meeting with the bride?

Just as all your advertising should focus on scheduling face-to-face visits, all of your presentations should focus on closing the sale. Everything in the presentation should be geared toward closing the sale. The goal of the presentation should not be to tell the bride about your product, but as you tell the bride about your product, you should be doing so in such a way as to make it easier for you to close the sale.

Many wedding professionals would say, "I met face-to-face with Diane and had a great time. We talked for an hour, and I really think she's going to book with us. I gave her all my information, and she was excited!"

Obviously, Diane wasn't that excited—she didn't commit to using your service! If the purpose of the presentation was to educate Diane or learn what Diane wanted, then I guess it was a success, but if the purpose of visiting with her face-to-face was to have her give you the initial investment on your fee, you failed!

I believe the purpose of the presentation, and every salesperson's job, can be summed up in three words:

Close the Sale

Just as your presentation should have a track to run on and an end goal of closing the sale, it's important to understand that there are some important emotional triggers that every bride-to-be has. In fact, all of us have them when we are considering a purchase, and many times, these emotional triggers are far more important than the price of the product we are looking at or the practicality of owning it.

I have a friend who owns a cake shop. Without a doubt, he is one of the best bakers in California. As with most business owners, my friend spends many hours each day running the store. It's not unusual for him to be at the shop at 8 a.m. and not go home until 9 p.m. On weekends, he's working all day Saturday, but occasionally, he will go through an entire Sunday without stopping by the shop. He works a lot.

About two years ago, he was driving by the Long Beach Convention Center on a Sunday and noticed it was having a boat show. Being spontaneous and thinking it would be fun, he decided to stop in. His wife thought it would be fun as well, so off to the boat show they went.

Three days later, my friend, who's never sailed a day in his life, was the proud owner of a 30-foot sailboat. It seems he decided while walking through the boat show that he was spending too much time at the shop. His solution was to store a significant amount of money in the form of a sailboat in a marina. Somehow, he felt if he spent a bunch of money on a boat, he would take time off work and use it.

When he told me the story about buying the boat, I asked him, "What made you invest $30,000 into a sailboat?" His answer was simple; he said, "I just wanted it." The more I spoke with the sales rep, the more I wanted it, and before I knew it I, they started calling me captain."

My friend ultimately did use the boat quite a bit and sailing has become a fun outlet for his entire family. Seems his theory worked, and he did start taking time off. However, let's look at what happened when he met with the boat salesman. The boat salesman understood the reason for the presentation. Everything he did during the presentation was designed to close the sale by doing one thing: create desire!

What Is Desire?

Have you ever seen a child, about 4 years old, who really wants something? She gets excited and jumps up and down. She squeals and yells, because she wants it so bad she can't control herself. If the child is that excited about getting a candy bar, how hard is it for the mom to get her to eat it?

Obviously, it's not hard at all. The mother has to do nothing more than give the child a nod, and the candy bar is gone.

When's the last time a bride felt that way about your service? Do brides get excited? Do they want to call all their friends and tell them about the great wedding service they just booked? If your clients are not excited when they book your service, why not? I'm not sure I understand. Most engaged women are first-time brides. They have had a vision of their wedding since they were young girls. They have just booked the photographer for the only wedding they plan on ever having, and they're not screaming for joy? It doesn't make sense to me.

What about the bride who keeps asking questions for three hours, and then, almost reluctantly, decides to use your service. Why did it take so long, and why isn't she excited?

Let's take a look at my good friends at the Walt Disney Company. The one thing I admire about the Walt Disney Company is that everything it does, it does well. If it's not done well, you never hear about it. I was once on a tour of MGM Studios in Florida, just before it opened to the public. The tour guide was taking us through some of the buildings and describing what the reason was that they were decorated the way they were. At one point, she said, "And the green you see on this wall is Mr. Eisner's favorite color. In fact, we originally painted it blue, but he changed it." We were surprised. Here, the CEO of a company the size of Walt Disney was involved in the selection of paint colors for a public area of MGM Florida. At first, I thought it was a little strange, but the more I thought about it, I realized that Michael Eisner had a vision of how that area should combine with the rest of the park to create excitement and help people have a great experience. If people have a great experience, they will be more likely to come back to MGM again. The wall color was a small part of creating a mood and, thereby, a desire to visit again.

If your brides aren't excited at your presentation, they don't have enough desire for your service. It's also true (and very cool) that when the bride is excited and she does have desire, she always invests in your service.

Sometimes, wedding professionals try to create desire the easy way. They think that by offering a wedding video along with the master tape for just $400 will entice every bride to use them. However, my experience has shown that while brides do consider price, they also want to have the wedding of their dreams. They will adjust the budget when there is enough desire.

Look at it this way: Do we buy what we need, or do we buy what we want? Even now, when the economy is suffering through a very tough time, most people don't walk into the thrift store and ask for the least expensive shirt. People still buy what they want, and what determines their degree of "want" is desire.

During your presentation, you will help the bride build desire for your service. Desire leads to want, and we all know what the bride wants, the bride gets.

How to Create Desire

There is a very easy system that I have taught thousands of people over the years that's going to help you build desire. This is simply a formula that I want you to use at every single presentation you perform. Wedding professionals have used this system over and over again, and thankfully, because most people have a tendency to react to similar situations in similar ways, it's successful more often than not.

Nothing is going to work 100 percent of the time. Many of the presentation skills we are going to discuss work well, but they will only move the desire meter a nudge, not a mile. If you have an overpriced, poorly implemented product that the bride can clearly see isn't worth the investment; your ability to create desire is going to be ineffective. For the sake of our discussion, I'm also going to assume the following:

- You believe you have the decision maker at the visit.
- You are in an area that's conducive to visiting with the bride.
- You're not trying to do nine things at once.
- Your cell phone is off.
- You have a brochure and a track to run on.
- Your product is professional.
- You're dressed appropriately.

If you can say yes to everything listed above, then we can move on, but before we do, I must take one minute to talk about cell phones. Just as the bride won't wait in line to meet you at a bridal show, she won't sit there while you answer 20 "important" calls. Asking her to look through pictures while you fight with a bride from six months ago about the balance on her account isn't going to create much desire—except the desire to escape.

Most cell phones have voice mail, and believe it or not, every text you receive doesn't have to be answered within 30 seconds. The cell phone used to be a useful tool. It's quickly becoming a huge time waster.

Features 101

Think about it this way: You have two new cars that look identical in every way. They are sitting on a car lot, side by side. As you look over the cars, you find that the one on the right has tons of features and the one on the left has nothing.

The car on the right has power steering, power brakes, electric windows, a GPS, and satellite radio. It has reclining seats, heated seats, an adjustable headrest, and cruise control. To top it off, it has a top-of-the-line built-in security system.

The one on the left doesn't have any of that. It has roll-up windows and cloth seats. It does have brakes, but that's about it. From the outside, they are identical. Now, answer these questions:

- Which one do you want?
- Which one will you enjoy more?
- Which car do you feel better about driving?
- Which car fits you better?

If you are like most people, you will want the car on the right. The car with all the features seems like a much better car. Even when the car on the right costs more than the one on the left, most people would want it. How do we know? Car manufacturers sell far more cars loaded with features than stripped-down cars with no features.

The car on the left is new, runs fine, and will get you where you want to go, but the dealership will sell 10 cars loaded with features for everyone that they sell that's stripped down.

People don't buy what they need; they buy what they want. How do we make them want? By giving them features!

What Is a Feature?

I've attended many seminars where the leader has spent tremendous amounts of time trying to define what a feature is. Usually, the speaker introduces some detailed chart that walks you through a process, and you ultimately arrive at a list of features.

I'm going to give you a slightly easier way to identify features. I believe a feature is anything about your product that you think is cool or you're proud of. If you're a wedding photographer, it can be the quality of your equipment or the way you dress at a wedding. Maybe it's the package you put together or the books you deliver the images in. A feature can be the fact that you shoot 300 images or the time you spend at a wedding.

You are the best person to decide what you feel is very cool about your service, so make a list of the top 10 features of your business.

1._____

2._____

3._____

4._____

5._____

6._____

7._____

8._____

9._____

10._____

Why 10 features? It's simple. I only want you to think about half of what you're ultimately going to need. That's right. You are going to eventually need to develop and memorize a list of 20 features of your product or service.

Now that you have developed a list of 10 features, I want you to take some time and create a description of each one. During my seminars, I find that people tend to say things like, "We're a full-service photographer." While I understand what that means because I have been in the business for many years, I promise, the bride doesn't have a clue about what that means. The most important part of having a list of features is being able to explain them in such a way that the bride understands.

Sometimes, it seems a little silly because the feature may be something like, "We wear tuxedos to every wedding." OK, so you wear a tuxedo. Now, explain it. That means you must explain what wearing a tuxedo to every wedding means. Why do you have to explain it? It's simple.

Have you ever had a time when you have said something to someone and they have nodded their head indicating they understood? Then, at some point later, you find out that they had no clue as to what you were talking about? This usually happens with children and employees. They look you right in the eye and agree, and then later, they do something exactly the way you asked them not to. When you ask them why they didn't do it the way you asked, they say, "Sorry, I didn't know that's the way you wanted it."

That's why you must name the feature and then describe or explain it—but we're not done yet. There is one more thing we have to do. We must tell the bride how it applies to her and explain the benefit.

We all have a little voice in the back of our heads asking, "So what?" When people tell us something, our little voice quickly determines if it applies to or affects us, and then helps us decide on our level of interest. When we hear things that we don't understand, our interest level is low; but when we hear about something that we do understand and why it applies to us, our interest meter goes even higher. The greater the interest, the more we want the feature.

There is a very easy way to share the benefit for a feature in a way the bride will understand. There are two magic words that help you along the way. They are "...so that...".

Let me show you how it works.

The Feature:

At every wedding, our entire team will be dressed in tuxedos.

Describe It:

It doesn't matter if we have two photographers or 20 at your wedding, they will all be dressed in the finest Pierre Cardin tuxedos that have been custom fit by one of the finest tailors in town.

The Benefit:

So that you never have to worry that the photographers will detract from you at your wedding by wearing some T-shirts with the company name on them or ill-fitted, worn-out tuxedos that they have worn to 600 other weddings.

You have a Feature – Description – Benefit. Having done seminars for many years, I understand that you have to say things so people understand them. When you put F.D.B. together, it's pronounced fudub. That's not good for people to remember, so many years ago, I changed it to: Feature – Advantage – Benefit, which is pronounced Fab and is much easier to remember. When we talk about Fab-ing brides, I really want you to fudub them, but you get the point.

Let's F.A.B.

Now it's time to take the 10 features we listed earlier and create the descriptions of those features.

1._____

2._____

3._____

4._____

5._____

6._____

7._____

8._____

9._____

10._____

The last step is to create the benefits description for each feature. Begin each line with "So that...."

1. So that_____

2. So that_____

3. So that_____

4, So that_____

5. So that_____

6. So that_____

7. So that_____

8. So that_____

9. So that_____

10. So that_____

You should now have a complete list of features, advantages, and benefits for 10 really great features of your product or service. Ultimately, you are going to need more, but for now, we're good to go.

With your bride in place, your cell phone off, and your features ready to go, it's time to start the presentation. There is an easy formula I follow during presentations, and while it's never exactly the same, it goes something like this:

- 5 minute introduction
- 35 minutes to learn about her vision
- 15 minutes to ask questions and present features to cover concerns
- 5 minutes to wrap up the paperwork

In reality, I'm closing the sale every minute of the presentation. When the bride says she hates something, I'm going to assure her we don't do that. When she loves it, we will make sure it happens. Once she has a chance to explain her vision, I present her with the features I believe will most accurately give her the wedding she has dreamed of. In the vast majority of cases, the presentation is over and done within one hour.

I love the Fab-ing part of the presentation best. That's the point where the bride starts to see how the features you're explaining have the ability to provide her with the wedding of her dreams. I have a list of about eight features that I start with and use those to build desire. If you're not providing features that excite brides, it's time to get new features.

There is also a very easy way to check with the bride to make sure she understands what you have said and to provide you with feedback as to how significant the bride believes certain features are.

How Does That Sound?

I simply explain a feature, advantage, and benefit and then ask, "How does that sound?" After talking with the bride and building rapport for the better part of 40 minutes, I promise, she's going to tell you how that sounds.

At some point, the bride is going to say, "This all sounds great!" At this point, you're going to forget about the rest of the features and close the sale. It's useless to keep telling the bride about 10 more features after she has said it sounds great. Look at it this way: She has been planning her wedding almost since birth, and she just told you that everything you have to offer sounds great. What more do you need? Shut up and close the sale!

Let's assume she says, "That doesn't sound good," or, "I don't like that." It's the perfect opportunity to say, "We've had a couple of brides feel the same way as you do. How can we adjust this to be exactly what you want?" The minute she starts helping you fill her needs, you are working together with a common mission: to create the wedding of her dreams!

How does that sound? It's great, isn't it?

CHAPTER 16 - Closing the Sale

Before I give you some powerful closings, I want to spend some time exploring some of the attitudes of wedding professionals when it comes to closing the sale. I believe there is a huge difference between helping a bride-to-be make a decision that is good for her and leading a bride-to-be into a decision that is bad for her.

For some reason, many wedding professionals appear to believe that selling a bride and, specifically, closing a sale is a bad thing. That explains why so many wedding professionals are so good at what they do but so bad at closing the sale. You must ask the bride-to-be to buy your product. If you don't attempt a close, you're cheating the bride-to-be. After all, when she selects your service, she's going to get the best possible product you can offer, isn't she? And you are going to help her have the wedding of her dreams, aren't you? Well, then, it simply makes sense that you cannot be afraid to ask the bride to take advantage of the opportunity you offer. If every bride who came through your door were a best friend, would you let her make decisions that are bad for her? Of course not! Help yourself by helping the bride and be sure to give every bride several opportunities to take advantage of your service. You must close the sale.

When is the Best Time to Close the Sale?

As I've discussed this question with wedding professionals, I've received a wide range of answers. Everything from, "I give every bride one hour, and if she hasn't bought, I let her go," to "I'm not comfortable being pushy with a bride, so I give her the information and let her decide." Unfortunately, many wedding professionals seem to think it's a good thing if you are not a great closer. I don't understand it, but I meet people all the time who tell me, "I don't push the bride to buy. I hate pushy sales people." Please don't mistake the pushy people who have tried to sell you things in the past with professional sales people. Their job title may have been salesperson, but if they beat you with a rubber hose or twisted your arm, they were not professional sales people; they were hacks.

The best time to close the sale is when you see the bride is ready. When you see the bride is:

- Excited and talking about your service
- Asking questions about how things work
- When things slow down after moving along well
- When you believe you have filled her needs and she's receptive

There are many times to close the sale. Don't get locked into a set presentation and miss the buying signals. When a bride is excited, invested, and interested, it's time to close the sale. Imagine you're visiting with a bride, and she says, "This is perfect. It's exactly what I want." You now have two options: You can keep talking and miss an opportunity, or you can say, "Well, I'm glad you feel that way, and we're excited about your wedding. Let me complete some information on the paperwork, and we will be on our way to helping you have the perfect wedding."

The bride may say, "Hold on. I'm not ready to place the order yet." In that case, you're going to say, "Mary, I find it easier to keep track of everything and organize my thoughts on the paperwork. That way, I won't forget anything." Then simply move on to the next feature or close. It's truly not a big deal, and I haven't ever heard of a bride who said, "This looks good..." while getting up and running out the door when the wedding professional attempted to close the sale.

Next, I want to discuss something all professional salespersons master, or they are not selling for very long. It's a technique that all of us should use more often, but because we try to control every situation, we don't. It's something that's very easy to do physically but, sometimes, a mental challenge. Learning how to do this one thing well will help you close many more sales.

Successful Silence

That's right. Successful silence is the ability to say to a bride-to-be, "Mary, I'm so happy you're excited about my cakes! What's the best time for us to deliver it on your wedding day, 9 a.m. or 10:30?" and then shutting your mouth.

Just sit there, nodding your head, with a smile on your face, waiting for the bride to respond. In sales, it's often said that the first one who talks after the close is set is the buyer. That means, if you set the close and then talk first, you've just bought your own product, and that's not a good thing.

You must master the art of not talking. Just sit, smile, and know that the first one who talks is the buyer.

The Assumed Close

This is most likely the close that most wedding professionals use 95 percent of the time. Unfortunately, it only works about 50 percent of the time.

The assumed close is simply when you find everything moving forward in a positive way. At some point, the bride stops saying "if" and starts saying "when". It can be 10 minutes into the presentation or 90 minutes, but you will know when it's right. Simply start filling in the paperwork. Eventually, you will complete it, and ask her to initial it. When she does that, you have a sale.

The most important part of using the assumed close is knowing when it's not working and it's time to move on to another technique. I've watched many wedding professionals blow through the entire presentation, feeling like they were spiritual matches for the bride-to-be, only to find out the bride wasn't that interested.

The easiest way to wrap up the assumed close is to say something like, "Diane, what's the best time to deliver the cake, 9:00 a.m. or 10:30?" When Dianne says, "9:30 is much better," simply say, "Great, just initial the paperwork, and I'll have our driver deliver the cake of your dreams at 9:30."

When she initials the paperwork and gives you the initial investment, you're done. Next sale please!

The "I Want to Think About It" Close

Have you ever had a bride say to you, "I want to think about it?" From this point forward, you're going to smile and know you're just a few minutes away from securing the order every time you hear a bride say, "I want to think about it."

The bride says something like, "Wow, John, your photography is great. Give me some time to think about it, and I'll get back to you." Or statements like:

- "We discuss everything before we decide."
- "Let us think it over."
- "I need to sleep on it."
- "Can I call you tomorrow?"
- "We never make decisions on the first appointment."

What the bride expects you to say is, "That's fine. Let me follow up in a few days." Many wedding professionals have a tendency to say just that, but you need to double our business in the next 12 months. You've already invested time in getting to know the bride, so you are not going to let her get away that easy. Obviously, you can't be rude, but you can't let her stop the sale by saying, "I want to think about it."

In your experience, what is it that the bride wants to think about? Is it that brides don't trust you, or they don't think you can perform as promised? Usually not. I've found that the vast majority of the time what the bride wants to "think about" is money. It's not always the money, but I'm sure that 95 percent of the time it is. At this point in the close, you can know two things:

1. The bride doesn't have enough desire. She's not jumping up and down and selling herself.

2. She probably wants to think about the money, but maybe not.

Many wedding professionals would say something to the bride like, "Well, Diane, what do you want to think about?" Then Diane will come up with some lame dodge designed to get her out the door as fast as possible. You simply can't be that aggressive if you are going to be a good closer. You need to be subtle, polite, and have your new friend help you out.

Understand, the vast majority of the time, the "I Want to Think About It" Close simply sets you up for the Reduction to the Ridiculous. That's because we know the majority of the time, the bride wants to think about the money. However, you just can't let her know that you know that yet.

Here's how it works:

The bride says, "I want to think about it."

You say, "Dianne, that's great. I certainly appreciate you taking the time to visit with me today."

At this point, she thinks she's off the hook, but you're just getting started. You go on: "And I know after having had a chance to get to know you that you are going to give this some serious thought, aren't you?"

She shakes her head and says yes, thinking it's over, but you continue on: "Diane, before you go, I would like to ask you to do me a favor. Will you help me understand exactly what it is that you want to think over? Is it the fact that…"

Now, notice—this is important—do not stop after the words "think over". If you stop there, you are dead. I've written it as a continuous sentence for a reason. If you stop at, "…what is it you want to think over," you are giving her permission to answer. But we don't want an answer yet.

By continuing on with, "Is it the fact that..." you now have a chance to start into your best features again, so have your best three features ready.

"Is it the fact that you don't think our cakes taste good?" Of course, she will say no. Then you say, "Is it the fact that you don't think we can deliver as promised?" Again, she will say no.

You can keep this up forever, but I suggest you bring up two or three of your best features—things you noticed she loved during the presentation. Finally, after she has said no a few times say, "Well, Diane, could it be the investment?"

Let's diagram it:

"Is it the fact that you don't think we can deliver as promised?" No.

"Is it that you're not sure our cake will taste good?" No.

"Is it something about the design you're unsure of?" No.

"Well, Diane, could it be the investment?" (Here, you stop talking.)

If it is the money, the vast majority of the time the bride will say yes. Smile, you're almost there.

What if Diane says, "No, it's not the investment"? What do you say to her then? In a loving and compassionate manner, it's okay to smile, and ask, "What is it?" More often than not, the bride is going to tell you what it is, and you say, "Thank you for sharing that. I know we can take care of that by..." And you fix her issue.

Then start closing all over again.

The Reduction to the Ridiculous

It's ridiculous how many ways you can use the reduction to the ridiculous. Simply put, the Reduction to the Ridiculous breaks whatever amount of money is concerning the bride down so far that the amount seems ridiculous. If you've ever seen an ad in the newspaper that says the new HD television is $3,400 or $89 per month, that's the Reduction to the Ridiculous. $3,400 is a bunch, but I can afford $89 a month, even if it is for 66 months. Does the Reduction to the Ridiculous work? You bet it does, and you need to have it in your closing arsenal.

It's important that when the bride says to you, "Your product costs too much," or "that's higher than I wanted to go" that you take a moment and clarify how much "too much" is. You see, as salespeople, we tend to look at the overall number, but the bride certainly didn't expect free photography for her wedding. So your $3,000 package may be more than she intended to invest, but it's not $3,000 too much.

Simply say, "Diane, I understand what you're saying. Today cost is certainly a concern for almost everything. Can you tell me about how much too much you feel it is?"

If Diane says she's seen similar packages for $2,500, the challenge isn't $3,000; it's now a much more manageable $500. That's what you focus on now, the smaller amount. Forget about the entire price at this point; focus on showing her the value she receives for the $500.

You say, "Diane, if I understand you correctly, we are really talking about $500, aren't we?"

She says, "Yes, your $500 too much."

At this point, I like to do a quick recap of two or three of my product's features we've discussed that I know are unique to me. I don't really give the bride a chance to speak yet, but I do want her to start seeing some of the features I have that my competitors don't.

Now you need to put it into the correct perspective. You can say, "Diane, let's work through this a little. Your wedding is how far away?"

She answers, "11 months."

"OK, 11 months is about 310 days, right?"

She says, "I guess."

"Diane, I was just trying to figure it out, because it seems to me if we spread that $500 over the next 310 days, we are really only talking about an investment of about $1.60 a day, right?"

She says, "I guess so."

"Diane, let me ask you one more thing. Won't the photography package we've designed offer you all of the images, quality, and expertise to provide you with images that are going to last you a lifetime? And having worked with you for a while, I can sense that this package really does offer the things you want for your wedding, doesn't it?

She says, "Yes, I think it will."

You say, "Great, we've agreed, haven't we? By the way, when is the best time to schedule your engagement sitting?"

The "No" Close

I love the "No" Close. I love it for the sheer audacity and boldness of the close. You have to be confident and sincere to use this close. Frankly, when I first was taught the "No" Close, I thought it was nonsense. I didn't think I would ever use it. Then I heard about Dennis Holt.

Dennis owned a company named Western Media. His company was founded on the theory that if an advertising agency gets a discount with radio and television stations, because they represent 10 clients, what type of discount would he get if he represented 10 advertising agencies. Over many years, he built Western Media into the largest advertising-buying service in the world. However, Dennis wasn't always the big guy on the block. In the beginning, he had to call on agency owners and fight for every bit of business. After all, there is a certain prestige to working with the network media outlets, and if the agencies went through Western, they feared losing some of the prestige.

Dennis called on one potential client who happened to be a major player in the advertising business. As they sat down to visit, the potential client started telling Dennis everything that was wrong with his concept. He went on for over 30 minutes, telling Dennis he was stupid and the idea was stupid. He used very profane language until the guy worked himself into such a frenzy that he ordered Dennis, who hadn't said three words, out of his office. On his way out the door, Dennis stopped, turned around, and said, "OK, I understand. I'm going to put you down as a firm maybe."

The guy he was meeting with screamed at him to get the hell out and Dennis left. A few years later, Dennis received a phone call from the same guy and asked if Western International would buy media for them. What I love about that story is in the face of all the bad things being thrown at Dennis, he kept his cool and knew that eventually this gentleman would work with him.

You have done the presentation. You have explained the features. You have tried the Assumed Close, the "I Want to Think About It" Close, and The Reduction to the Ridiculous. In fact, you have tried everything—even creating closes on the spot, because you want this sale and it's just not happening. The bride continues to say no.

Understand, at this point, you don't have much to lose. It's not like three minutes after leaving you she's going to decide she was wrong. Take a breath, put on your most caring attitude, and have some fun. Launch the "No" Close.

Here's what you say:

"Diane, I appreciate the time you have taken here today to visit with me. I have enjoyed getting to know you, and frankly, I appreciate the opportunity to build a friendship with you. I think I understand what you want your wedding to be, and if I'm not mistaken, we have created a wedding photography package that fills every one of your needs, So I'm a little concerned that having been together this long and working together as we have, that if you select any other photography service, you won't receive exactly what you want. I never let my friends make a mistake when I can prevent it. So, Diane, I have to say I can't accept your no. I can't risk you not having the perfect wedding photography I know I can deliver. Diane, it can't be a no, it has to be yes!"

Stop Talking – Sit – Smile - Enjoy

I know. It sounds strange, but believe me, once you have a chance to try it, it's amazing how about 25 percent of the time you save the sale. You must be strong. You must be sincere, and remember, there isn't a thing wrong with helping a bride decide to do business with you. You are going to give her the best possible product and service, and when she deals with you, you will know she is getting the best. Don't be afraid. Close with gusto.

One last resource I want to remind you about is Tom Hopkins Book, *How to Master the Art of Selling*. Tom's book will provide you with 16 great closes as well as fantastic information that will make you into a sales champion. I have used Tom's selling techniques for years, and I have been able to have a lifestyle and career that is better than I thought possible. Purchasing *How to Master the Art of Selling* will be a great investment. After all, it's the second best book about selling I know of! ☺

CHAPTER 17 - Making All Your Advertising Successful

The number of face-to-face visits a particular type of advertising generates is the gold standard by which you should measure all your advertising success. Once you are happy with the number of face-to-face visits, you should start advertising programs for secondary goals, such as branding or educational awareness.

There are other important facets of advertising that need to be understood to ensure advertising success.

Reach vs. Frequency

This is a core-advertising concept that's important for the wedding professional to understand. When you purchase advertising, no matter what type of advertising, you may need to make a decision regarding what the frequency of the advertising will be and what the reach of the advertising will be. Due to limited advertising budgets, in most cases, you don't have the luxury of having both reach and frequency. In fact, in many cases, it's important to have one but not the other.

Advertising Frequency

We've all heard it said that the average customer has to hear your message a set number of times before responding. Over the years, as we've worked with wedding professionals, the number has changed. Originally, it was commonly thought that if a customer heard your message three to five times, she would respond. More recently, I saw a study done by the national Chamber of Commerce that showed that because people are hit so often with advertising messages now that the actual number of times a person has to see your message has dramatically increased to nine times before responding.

It make sense to me that the number of times a person has to hear your message has increased, because we are now bombarded with advertising messages all day long. Twenty-five years ago, the average person received less direct mail advertising and no e-mail advertising; advertising was limited to the major TV networks, radio stations, newspapers, and magazines.

Now, you can't go into a restaurant and look at the menu without seeing the little advertising squares around the edge. Go into your local car wash, and as your car's being washed, chances are, you're going to have a board with 50 or 100 business cards where people have paid to have their business card placed on display. Even your local grocery store has found that it can derive a few more pennies in profit each month by selling advertising on the shopping cart you use or on the back of receipts. In addition, I believe it's a fact that as we are inundated with more and more forms of advertising, we become desensitized to the messages that that advertising contains.

Envision our friendly bride-to-be; she has just accepted the proposal of her boyfriend, now her fiancé, John. She's on cloud nine. She is about to be married to the greatest man in the world, and her future is bright. Studies have shown that from the moment a woman accepts a marriage proposal until the day of her wedding, she spends 45 percent of her time planning her wedding. With an average 16-month engagement, that means she is going to spend over 1,200 hours planning her wedding. During most of that time, she is going to be bombarded with messages from wedding professionals.

It makes sense that to cut through the clutter you need to have your message delivered to the prospect more frequently than in the past. For most wedding professionals, the frequency of your message delivery is more important than the reach of your message.

Advertising Reach

The reach of your message is another easy concept to understand, but tough to master. Reach simply speaks to how many people hear your message. It's important to analyze each form of advertising to determine what the reach is for that medium. For example, it doesn't make much sense for a small, one-location, formal wear rental store to advertise in the magazine that may have a reach of 45,000 brides when 95 percent of those brides are located more than 25 miles away from the store. The reach number of 45,000 is impressive, but the target area is not so impressive.

Most wedding professionals should concentrate on the frequency of their message. Working to ensure that the bride received your message in a timely and frequent manner several times is going to be more effective than worrying about reaching 300,000 brides at once with your message.

Targeting Your Advertising

You certainly don't need me to tell you that you are better off buying an advertisement in a wedding magazine than you are in a hunting magazine. Few, if any, wedding professionals would invest in such advertising, because you know that while you may get a customer every now and then, for the same amount of money, in a more targeted advertising outlet, you would reap greater rewards.

I have a friend who years ago learned the importance of targeting his advertising message. He formed a company on a whim with a friend of his. They visited some of the lumber processing mills by the redwood sequoias in California and purchased a bag of giant seeds. Now this bag was really more of a sack. It contained literally millions of giant redwood sequoia tree seeds. My friend and his associate formed a company called Rolzarri Enterprises. They came up with the name because one of them wanted to purchase a Rolls Royce, and the other wanted a Ferrari. Thus, their company name became Rolzarri. They purchased advertising in the National Enquirer. They ran a beautiful ad that featured the drawing of a giant redwood sequoia, and it read, "Leave a living heirloom for all time. Order giant redwood seeds and plant them in your yard."

Frankly, I think they anticipated that they were wasting their money. They invested $1,300 in the National Enquirer. They sold the seeds in packets of 10 seeds for $19.95. It was amazing to see the orders pour in. This was long before the Internet, so the only way to receive orders was via the mail. Over a period of about six weeks, they received hundreds of orders from all over the country. They received orders from every single state, including Alaska and Hawaii, as well as Puerto Rico. Buoyed by their success and the profit they had made, they decided to expand their advertising message and reach out to more people. They purchased an advertisement in a very popular gardening magazine at a charge substantially more than the National Enquirer, but based on the success they had, they felt confident there was a solid investment. Six weeks after placing their second ad, they had received a total of no orders from their gardening magazine ad. You see, people who read gardening magazines know more about growing giant redwood trees than those who read the National Enquirer. Many of the people who read the gardening magazine probably knew that there is a reason why giant redwood trees grow predominantly in one place on the planet. It's certainly possible to start and grow one anywhere. However, is it practical to plant a tree in your front yard that someday may be 250 feet tall and 65 feet wide? Not to mention, the fact that it may take somewhere in the area of 2,000 years for the tree to grow to its full height, and it would obliterate any house that was near its base, didn't go unnoticed by those who purchased the gardening magazine.

My friend learned a valuable lesson about targeting his advertising. When he reached people who did not know much about growing redwoods but who respected their beauty, the sales did well. When he reached a more educated crowd, who understood some of the dynamics of growing giant redwoods, his sales did not do well.

Outbound Calls - Calling for Dollars

Let's face it. Telemarketing isn't for everyone. Some people hate the thought of calling people, who are at home eating dinner, and bugging them about whatever it is they are selling. I once knew an insurance agent that went to his boss and said, "I hate calling people and interrupting their dinner." The Sales Manager said, "OK, don't call them at dinner time!" The problem was solved.

If you ask, most brides that register in your booth with you will give you a work number or a cell number. I find it's much easier to reach the bride at work, and if it weren't appropriate for you to call her, she wouldn't have given you the number. Regardless, I always start by asking, "Can we visit for a minute?" I've never had a bride stop me at 60 seconds and say, "Time's up! Goodbye!"

It's also critical that when you call the brides you understand what the one and only goal of the call is: to book a face-to-face visit. Just like all other forms of advertising, it's important to understand the goal and always work towards that. Here's the perfect script to use once you have the bride on the phone and she's said it's ok to talk. If her name is Diane, I'm going to take a big breath, and say:

"Diane, this is Chris. I own Chris' Flowers. We had a chance to visit for a minute at the bridal show, and I'm following up on that. Here at Chris' Flowers, we specialize in one-on-one attention with every bride we work with. In order to do that, we need to sit down and talk so that you can tell me about your dream wedding. Obviously, we can't do that over the phone, so I am calling to find out when will be the best time to schedule a face-to-face visit so that we can talk about your wedding— mornings or afternoons?"

Never ask a question that the bride can say yes or no to. Every question should offer an either/or answer. When you use this script, it's very possible the bride will come back with an answer like:

"I don't remember seeing you at the show; there were so many florists. How much do your wedding packages cost?"

Later in the book, I'm going to give you an extensive look into how to answer most questions and objections, but for this specific call, I would answer Diane's question like this:

"Diane, I get that question quite a bit, and the truth is we have floral packages that start at as little as a hundred dollars and go into the thousands. I'm calling today, because one of the things I'm most proud of about my business is that we specialize in making brides' dreams come true. We can work within almost any budget, and truthfully, the only thing I want to do in the beginning is to find out what your vision is for your wedding. Once I know that, I'm confident we can make your dream come true and stay within your budget. When is the best time to schedule a face-to-face visit so that we can talk about your wedding— mornings or afternoons?"

Do not attempt to sell your service in the telephone call. Your primary objective should be to secure the face-to-face visit. It's inevitable that some brides will start asking questions or throw something at you that you didn't expect, but stay on task and go for the face-to-face visit. Here are some general calling guidelines:

Pre-Call Planning

Have a primary objective for every telemarketing call, defined as, *What do I want them to DO as a result of this call, and what do I want to do?*

Prepare questions for your call using your call objective. Ask yourself, *How can I persuade them to take this action as a result of asking questions?* Remember, people believe more of their ideas than yours.

Have a secondary objective for each telephone sales call, something you'll strive to accomplish every time. Pick something you'll have a good chance to succeed with, such as, getting their agreement that they will accept literature if they won't schedule a visit. This way, you can enjoy success on every call, and that does wonders for your attitude.

If leaving a message on voice mail, be certain it offers a hint of a benefit/result that sparks curiosity, but doesn't talk about products/services.

Use the script and don't use silly, resistance inducing phrases on your telesales call, like, "If I could show you a way to _____, you would, wouldn't you?" The only decision you're looking for from the call is to schedule a face-to-face visit with you.

When cold call prospecting, don't start the call with, "I was just calling people who attended the recent bridal show..." People want to feel like they're the only person you're calling... not just one of the masses from a list of compiled names. Try, "I'm calling you because you were at the bridal show."

Avoid asking go-nowhere questions like, "Is everything going OK?" "What are your needs?" "Are you having any problems now?" "How's the wedding coming?" and, "What is your budget?" These all force the person to think too much.

Always know where you'll go with answers, regardless of the question. In other words, have a call plan and stick to it. She may say she's a month behind schedule and 50% over budget, but that doesn't mean you should not push for the face-to-face visit.

Resist the tendency to present. Some reps get so excited when they hear the slightest hint of an opportunity that they turn on the spigot of benefits. Hold off. Ask a few more questions, get better information. Do this and you'll be able to craft an even harder-hitting description of benefits, tailored precisely to what they're interested in and presented during the face-to-face visit.

Learn more about the decision-making process. There could be many behind-the-scenes influences on the decision. Ask who's helping with the wedding, and when scheduling the visit, ask who should be there.

Inbound Calls - Answering for Dollars

Understanding the primary reason to participate in bridal shows is to schedule face-to-face visits, and the primary reason to telephone the bride-to-be after the show is to schedule face-to-face visits.

What would you guess the primary reason to answer your telephone is? The primary reason to answer the telephone in your business is to schedule face-to-face visits. You may be wondering how that's possible; after all, the bride rarely calls and says, "Let's book a face-to-face visit." Typically, she calls and asks something like, "How much is your service?" For some reason, I still meet wedding professionals who are frustrated when the bride-to-be calls and only seems to be interested in how much the service is. The problem is they have forgotten that people don't buy what they can afford; they buy what they want. So why do brides always seem to ask about the price of a service first? If it wasn't important, why would they ask?

Why the Bride Asks About Money

Do you remember when you were a child and your mother would give you some lunch money for school? I'll bet your mother would give you the money and say something like, "Keep that in your pocket, and don't lose it." You would push the money into your pocket and breathe a sigh of relief when you gave it to the teacher, knowing that you had made it to school and you didn't lose the money. We have all been taught that we need to protect our money.

Another thing we have been told since we were children is "there's no such thing as a stupid question". But we all know that's not true. How many times have you sat in a meeting, heard someone ask a question, and thought to yourself, *Thank God I didn't ask that question; it's stupid!* We've all done it. Even if you don't want to admit it, I know you've done it to!

We now have a bride calling a wedding photographer for the first time in her life. She knows nothing about wedding photography, but she does know that protecting her money is good, and she shouldn't ask a stupid question. Is it any wonder the first question she asks is, "How much money does it cost?" She's protecting her money, and that's never stupid. In the outbound calling section, I gave you a script to use in this situation.

When brides call into your business, your primary goal should be to ask every bride for a one-on-one visit. It's no different than calling out. When the bride calls you and asks, "Do you have purple roses with red stems," your answer should be:

"If you want purple roses with red stems, we will find a way to make that happen. In fact, here at Chris' Flowers, we specialize in one-on-one attention with every bride we work with. In order to do that, we need to sit down and talk so you can tell me about your dream wedding. Obviously, we can't do that over the phone, so when will be the best time to schedule a face-to-face visit so that we can talk about your wedding—mornings or afternoons?

Inbound, outbound—it doesn't matter. It's all about scheduling face-to-face visits with the bride-to-be.

Making Print Advertising Work

Print advertising has its place. It is obvious from our prior examples that print advertising cannot produce the number of face-to-face visits, because you have to rely on them calling into your location. However, most print advertising has the distinct advantage of reaching a large audience.

Some wedding magazines will easily reach an audience five or ten times the size of a bridal show. Much of enhanced reach advantage is lost when you consider that you will have one page out of hundreds, but wedding magazines can still be productive for the wedding professional.

The way to make your print advertising work is to create an ad, based on the guidelines already discussed, that offers a distinct opportunity if the bride responds quickly. Chances are, you can look through many wedding magazines, and you will find page after page of reception location advertising that simply shows the location and doesn't do much more.

This type of ineffective, non-targeted advertising won't work for the average wedding professional. Remember, your print advertising, like all advertising, should be judged by the number of opportunities it provides you to sell your product face-to-face with the bride. Your print ads should be designed to stimulate the bride to pick up the phone and call you.

Making Direct Mail Work

As with all advertising, your direct mail piece should stimulate the bride to call you. That means that the information in that mail piece should be focused towards that single goal.

Direct mail can be an important part of your advertising campaign. When a correctly formatted mailing piece is mailed to a targeted list, you can reap significant rewards. I've included a complete Bonus Chapter about direct mail, because it can be so instrumental in your success.

Make Your Web Page Work

I've dedicated an entire chapter to the discussion about your web page. This is another topic that requires a complete book just to scratch the surface, but as useful and wonderful as the web is and as much as it's a time saver and has eliminated continents and time zones around the world, the Internet and your web page don't offer the immediate one-on-one interface you need to close your sales.

Think about this: As I'm writing this book, I've been communicating through Instant Message on Yahoo with my radio show producer in Hawaii, my web guy in India, my database manager in Columbia, my script writer for my television segments in New Zealand, and all five members of my staff, who are nowhere near me. Ten years ago, we had a staff of fifteen all locked in the same office each day, doing what we needed to do to stay busy. Now, because of the Internet, we do more work with less staff, and we are literally spread out all over the world. The Internet and the web is amazing, it just may not be as useful as you think.

The Internet does offer volume and reach. You can easily have a bride in Poland review your site and even send you an email with twenty questions. Next time you have a wedding in Poland, it may be helpful.

Blogging for Brides

Earlier, we discussed social networking, so I won't belabor the point. Blogging is all the rage. Now we can find out what every friend is doing every minute of every day. Some people are fascinated by it. I appreciate the technology, and I marvel at the truly wonderful things the Internet offers. I must admit I don't fully appreciate why people seem so intent upon sharing the most intimate parts of their lives with the world, but social networks are a great way to reach out to this tech savvy generation. This requires you to have a presence on Facebook, Myspace, Twitter, and any other web service that provides an opportunity for you to reach out to brides. Like all advertising, the social networking sites should be viewed as a way to generate face-to-face visits. Just as the telephone allows a person to reach into your business and gather information, social networking sites allow the bride to communicate with you and start building rapport.

The key to successful use of blogging and social networking sites is to provide enough information that the bride is interested in communicating with you, but not so much that she doesn't have to contact you. As you communicate with the bride-to-be, be sure to explain the same basic information that you would when they call on the phone. She may be ready to provide you (and 50 others) with every detail of what she wants, and she may even badger you for a firm price, but know when to say no.

Blog with the bride until your heart's content, but the minute she starts asking about prices, terms, and conditions, you're always better off scheduling a face-to-face visit. Besides, it's fun to meet someone you have been talking to via the Internet.

CHAPTER 18 – Bringing It All Together

I've made you one simple promise. You can double your wedding business in the next 12 months. This is the point where we pull everything together and start the work of doubling your business.

Reaching your goal may require some drastic changes to the way you do business. I'm confident that the rewards will far outweigh the challenges, and having twice as much income and profit will provide you and your family with the benefits you deserve for taking on this challenge.

Let's start by clarifying my position on advertising. I believe there are many ways you can advertise your business to build name recognition, branding, and credibility. Many of the advertising sources discussed in this book are excellent for those purposes, but our goal is to **double your business in the next 12 months**. To do that, we have to concentrate on *only* those methods that allow you the best opportunity to reach your goal.

Bridal shows happen to be the one advertising source that offers you the fastest opportunity for a high rate of return. It's not that the promoters or the shows are special; it's the fact that you get to meet prospects face-to-face and control the sales environment from the beginning to the end. In effect, it's not the show or promoter that makes the show successful. It's *your* effort and the one-on-one access that makes the show successful.

Let's recap. We agree:

1. The amount of money you put in your checking account is directly related to the number of sales you make.
2. The amount of sales you make is directly related to the number of presentations you perform.
3. The number of presentations you perform is directly related to the number of face-to-face visits you set.
4. The number of face-to-face visits you set is a direct result of the number of times you ask a prospect to visit with you.

5. Your advertising should focus primarily on giving you an opportunity to ask brides to visit with you.

6. The only form of advertising that provides you with a chance to meet a bride-to-be in person is a bridal show.

For the next year, your primary advertising should be (in order of priority):

- Bridal shows
- Direct mail to pre-show and post-show lists
- Email to pre-show and post-show lists
- Your web page and networking
- Networking and referrals from other wedding professionals
- Small, informational ads in wedding magazines

Steps to Take to Double Your Business

1. Review Chapter 2. Develop a fixed amount that signifies what it would take to double your business in the next year.

2. Create a comprehensive piece of literature to be used during presentations. Highlight ten primary and ten secondary features about your product.

3. Join at least two business-networking groups. Reach out to two wedding professionals each week that you do not know.

4. Train your staff to ensure that they understand that their primary job, before everything else, is to sell product and service the customer.

5. Create scripts for every employee and require them to follow the script, word for word, during all outbound and inbound calls. Post the scripts by all phones. Be diligent

and do not allow anyone to change the script unless you approve the change.

6. Cancel any advertising that doesn't create opportunities for you to meet brides face-to-face. I understand that every wedding advertising source is going to say this doesn't make sense, but they are wrong. We are going to concentrate on ONLY the advertising that delivers brides face-to-face.

7. Contact every wedding professional you know and set-up a cross referral program. Make sure you have their literature and they have yours. Track what professionals refer you most and be sure to reward them.

8. Replace any non-effective business verbiage with phrases you currently use with the verbiage and phrases discussed in Chapter 4.

9. Buy Tom Hopkins Book, *How to Master the Art of Selling*, for each staff member and make it mandatory reading. Require one chapter each week with tests on Fridays.

10. Form a list of bridal shows that will be held in your marketing area over the next 12 months. Place reservations for one booth in each show that has attendance of over 500 brides the year before.

11. Request a pre-event list of brides from the bridal show promoters. Email and Snail Mail a postcard prior to the show.

12. Do a general announcement three times a week, starting one month before the show on Twitter, Facebook, Myspace, and any other social networking sites you are a part of, announcing your booth number and inviting people to the show.

13. Prepare your booth according to the booth design guidelines.

14. Work each show with the sole intent of setting face-to-face visits. Follow the guidelines from Chapter 13.

15. Schedule visits with wedding professionals you haven't met before—network, network, network

16. Design your presentation and supply list a minimum of fifteen days before the show and rehearse the presentation with staff in front of mirror.

17. Contact the show producer and explore ways to have your company logo placed in significant spots around the show and on the fashion show stage.

18. Set a specific goal for each show as to how many bridal visits and wedding professional visits you want to schedule.

19. After the show, follow up as outlined in Chapter 13.

20. Follow the directions in Chapter 15 for the perfect presentation.

21. Review Chapter 16 and close every sale.

I've seen thousands of wedding professionals invest millions of dollars in marginal advertising. Much of the problem was the wedding professional didn't understand how to make their advertising successful. In order to do that, you need to immediately increase your face-to-face visits with brides and start conducting more presentations. My system will work, but much of the problem was also because the sales representatives for the advertising source were more interested in selling advertising than helping the wedding professional make sales.

Just as it's not enough to place an ad in a wedding magazine and expect huge returns, it's not right that the person selling the advertising takes your money and leaves your success up to you. You need to invest in advertising that works. You need to know what will and will not help you, and most of all, you need to keep focused on what makes you successful.

You now have everything you need to get started. I truly believe you can double your wedding business by following my guidelines.

In the event that you do need additional assistance, be sure to communicate with me directly by telephone, fax, or email at www.EvansSalesSolutions.com.

Until we have an opportunity to talk again,

Good Luck, God Bless, and Happy Selling!

My Story – Part 4

The third meeting of the people who were working to form the Bridal Show Producers International was held in Las Vegas in 1996. A smaller group of show producers met three days before the general meeting to iron out some by-laws and some type of structure to the association. There were several large and small producers present— Richard Markel from Sacramento, David Gafkey and Bill Brennan from Chicago, Tommy Vaughn from Atlanta, Bruce Theibauth from Minnesota, Dale Tomay from Northern California, and Anne Nolla and Sharon Sacks from San Jose, California. I represented Southern California. Brad Buckles was from Seattle, and Josh Franz was from Minneapolis. Debbie Hansen was from Las Vegas, and Jerry Russo was from Royal Prestige.

Jerry has supported the BSPi since day one as an Associate Member. In fact, Debbie and her husband provided all of the sound equipment and presentation gear we needed to have a meeting of 15-20 people for three days and 65-70 for three more. It was a meeting like no other. You ultimately had over 60 bridal show producers, whom in the past had worked independently, coming together to form an association and improve the bridal show business for exhibitors. The show producers wanted to work together to insure that every exhibitor received a quality show, and that the producers could help each other to insure show success. It was a super idea, and Richard deserves the credit for it.

As with anything that you turn over to others, the BSPi took on a life of its own. Richard did not become the Director of the BSPi as he had planned. I was elected to the position, and after being assured by Richard that he truly did want the group to make the choice, I accepted and served for four years. We consistently worked to provide the resources for the association to get better by providing training, product information, and education and simply getting together to talk. It was a great group with noble intentions. In 1999, at the end of my time as Director, I left the group, wishing them much success, and while I still stay in touch with many of the good friends I made at the BSPi, I found that the group as a whole was moving towards fewer members, protected areas, and less competition among promoters. In effect, people were protecting their areas from others instead of helping newer promoters become better. There is certainly nothing wrong with the group or their mission; it's just different than we had originally planned.

In 2005, I formed the Bridal Show Producers of America—a much smaller group of show promoters who meet once each year and discuss ways to improve shows. The main qualifier for membership in Bridal Show Producers of America is that you must want to make your show better. To qualify for membership, you need nothing more than a desire to produce great shows.

From 2000 to present, I have expanded our show offering. Our shows now include women's shows, fitness shows, Green Living Expo's, and green concerts. I've found that through it all, one thing remains constant: Many businesses believe that investing in advertising and trade shows is important, but few, if any, have any set idea of what success is.

I've seen wedding businesses that were million dollar companies completely blow their advertising budget with nothing to show for it, and I've seen fantastic business people with the strangest products do well because they had a plan. We had a lady at the Torrance Marriott Bridal Expo who sold vacuum cleaner covers that were sewed to look like brides and grooms. That's right—a vacuum cleaner cover. We don't usually offer half booths, but I sold her only half a booth. She was mad. She wanted a full booth. However, I didn't want to take her money, only to have her booth become a failure. Much to my surprise, she did fantastically. She sold more vacuum cleaner covers than she had, and she had to take orders!

She had a plan, a mission, and a goal, and she stuck to it. That's my goal for you. Now that we are reaching the end of the book, I want to encourage you to have a plan. Set goals. Measure the goals for success and adjust as needed. It's important not to allow your business to run on autopilot. There is a time for that, but not if you are trying to make your business grow!

Currently, I work with many show producers and wedding professionals throughout the nation, helping them coordinate and run their business. I work with companies, both small and large, and help them grow their business.

BONUS CHAPTER 1 – Direct Mail Secrets

Successful direct mail doesn't depend on cool graphics, four-color printing, or edgy copy. I've found that 99% of the mistakes made in direct mail can be classified into a few areas. Here's a complete list, followed by specific detail.

- Not using direct mail
- No reply card
- Mailing to a bad list
- Not testing
- Selling features not benefits
- Not having an offer
- Making a bad offer

The wedding professionals I've met who use direct mail, seldom track response or test one mailing piece or list against another. Unfortunately, that means they repeat their past failures and have no idea of what works in direct mail—and what doesn't. It's a big mistake.

Not Using Direct Mail

We've already reviewed the success rate of direct mail in our advertising evaluation worksheet. When your product margin is high enough to insure you will make profit from a 1% response, direct mail makes sense. As email becomes harder to deliver because of spam filters and new laws designed to encroach upon businesses using email to promote their business, direct mail delivered to a prospect's mailbox is experiencing a renewed success. What used to be considered junk mail is now being noticed more than ever. You should have a consistent direct mail program.

No Reply Card = No Sale

Virtually every piece of direct mail should contain a reply card. If it's a letter and a number 10 envelope, it's easy to include a reply card, and while this type of mailing is the least effective, it may become virtually useless if you don't include a reply card.

The four most common types of direct-mail pieces are: postcards, number 10 envelopes with a letter, an oversized envelope with a letter, or a catalog. The Direct-Mail Marketing Association conducted a study and found that the most commonly read and, therefore, most successful direct mail pieces were as follows:

- Postcards were the most commonly read piece of direct mail.
- Catalogs were the second-most read piece of direct mail.
- Oversized envelopes were opened and read the third highest of the four pieces.
- And the least read piece of direct mail was a number 10 envelope with a letter inside.

Interestingly enough, when you evaluate these four forms of direct mail, it's easy to see that the direct mail piece that represents the smallest investment is the postcard, followed by the number 10 envelope, the oversized envelope, and then the catalog. So, a postcard is the most read piece of direct mail and the least expensive to mail. That makes it a substantial value for any wedding professional.

You may be asking yourself, *Is it possible to include a reply card with a postcard?* And the answer might surprise you. Not only can you design and produce a postcard with a reply card (as shown in the picture below), but it will cost you no greater amount of postage to mail a postcard with a reply card than it does to mail a regular postcard. That's why successful wedding professionals know that postcards are a super value when it comes to reaching out to a qualified list to brides.

Mailing to a Bad List

Do you know what the most important part of your direct mail campaign is? It's not the artwork or the copy. It's not the size of the mailing piece or when you mail it. It's the mailing list.

A great mailing package, with superior copy and great design, might pull double the response of a poorly designed mailing. However, the best list can pull a response 10 times more than the worst list for the identical mailing piece.

The most common direct mail mistake is not investing enough time and money, when you select and then test the right lists. Remember, in direct marketing, a mailing list is not just part of your mailing program. It is "the" program.

Fortunately, there are ample supplies of quality mailing lists for the wedding industry. The wedding professional just has to know how to cut through the advertising hype and select the proper list or how to develop and maintain a list on his or her own.

Not Testing

Big mailers test all the time. Some of the larger mailers test just about everything—even the size and shape of the indicia on the outer envelope.

Wedding professionals, on the other hand, seldom track responses or test one mailing piece or list against another.

As a result, they repeat their failures and have no idea of what works in direct mail—and what doesn't. In direct mail, you should not assume you know what will work. You should test it to find out.

For example, a copywriter wrote a subscription package for California Bride magazine. His mailing became the "control" package for 5 years. That is, no mailing piece tested against it brought back as many subscriptions.

The envelope teaser and theme of that successful mailing was "15 Ways to Have the Perfect Wedding". Yet, it's easy to see that if that exact same promotional line was used to for other magazines, such as *Good Housekeeping, Readers Digest,* or *Inc. Magazine,* the results would be much different.

You don't know whether something will work until you test it. And you cannot predict test results based on past experience.

Selling Features Not Benefits

Perhaps the oldest and most widely embraced rule for writing direct-mail copy is, "Stress benefits, not features." But in business-to-business marketing, that doesn't always hold true.

In certain situations, features must be given equal (if not top) billing over benefits.

For example, if you've ever advertised semiconductors, you know that design engineers are hungry for specs. They want hard data on drain-source, voltage, power dissipation, input capacitance, and rise-and-fall time—not broad advertising claims about how the product helps save time and money or improves performance.

"I've tested many mailings selling engineering components and products to OEMs (Original Equipment Manufacturers)," says Don Jay Smith, president of the Chatham, NJ-based, ad agency, The Wordsmith. "I've found that features and specs out pull benefits almost every time."

In the same way, I suspect that doctors are swayed more by hard medical data than by advertising claims, and that industrial chemists are eager to learn about complex formulations that the average advertising writer might reject as "too technical."

In short, the copywriter's real challenge is to find out what the customer wants to know about your product—and then tell him in your mailing.

Not Having an Offer

An offer is what the reader gets when he responds to your mailing. To be successful, a direct-mail package should sell the offer, not the product itself. For example, if I mail a letter describing a new video montage option, my letter is not going to do the whole job of convincing people to buy my service. But the letter is capable of swaying some people to at least show interest by requesting a free brochure or more information about the video montage.

Make sure you have a well-thought-out offer in every mailing. If you think the offer and the way you describe it are unimportant, you are wrong.

Making a Bad Offer

A catering facility in Malibu, California, ran a direct mail piece with the following offer:

"Visit the Malibu Sea Lion and receive a free appetizer when you book your reception."

While attending a seminar that I taught, they asked me to review their mailer and comment on it. At first, I thought the offer was adequate, because I believed that they were offering a free additional serving of appetizers when a bride booked their service. It wasn't until they explained that their offer was "a" free appetizer that I realized this was probably the worst offer I had ever seen. In effect, they were saying, "Drive 25 miles to our facility, and we will give you a weenie on a toothpick"—not a compelling offer.

Here are some effective offers for industrial direct mail: free brochure, free report, free analysis, free consultation, free demonstration, free trial use, free catalog, etc.

Your copy should concentrate on increasing the reader's desire to send for whatever it is you offer. For example, a catalog becomes a product guide. A collection of brochures becomes a free information kit. A checklist becomes a convention planner's guide. An article reprinted in pamphlet form becomes "our new, informative booklet." Only use copy that builds desire for the offer. It doesn't matter that you have been in business for 30 years. On the mailing piece, you only want to say what you need to in order to get them to respond to your offer.

BONUS CHAPTER 2 – Ten Web Mistakes You Shouldn't Make

How to Block Your Customers

I believe, many wedding professionals completely miss the point of email, and it's costing them business. First, let me establish the fact that I do not enjoy receiving spam email. I have several websites with my email address posted throughout the Internet, so I receive a ton of spam. It's not uncommon for me to receive somewhere between 200 and 600 emails every day. About 95 percent of the emails are spam, so unsolicited email has a daily impact upon my business. I understand that, but I also understand that receiving unsolicited email is a fact of life. Just like receiving advertising in my office mailbox each day, it's not going to stop, and frankly, it shouldn't.

I'm amazed by the response many wedding professionals have taken to prevent unwanted email. Many act as if receiving spam email is virtually destroying their business, and there is nothing more important than stopping it in any way possible. They erect barrier after barrier to insure no piece of email ever hits their desktop as if the computer would blow-up if it did. Unfortunately, the filters, barriers, and spam blocking services also have a tendency to block something else: your customers or, worse yet, potential customers.

When a bride to be sends you an email and then receives a message back that says something like, "Hello, I'm protecting myself from unwanted email. Please enter your name in the box below to prove you're a human. Once that is done, I will receive your email."

Forget for the moment that the potential customer may not see your return message (because it may get lost in her spam filter,) but what are you really saying to the bride-to-be? I believe when a bride-to-be receives spam filter message like the one above, she thinks, "Wow, it's more important for this company to save 15 seconds of time than it is to see my message. I'm not a spammer. These guys are crazy." Off she goes, never to contact you again.

The spam filtering services have a place. They are great at protecting personal email boxes for individuals who don't know how to do it themselves. For the average wedding professional who is (let's face it) a wedding business, a spam filter service that blocks you from your potential clients until they are cleared is nonsense. It is not incumbent upon the bride-to-be to get your permission to send you a message.

Remove the spam blockers and set-up some common sense filters that every email program offers. Then, spend 5 minutes a day clearing your messages and get on with marketing your business.

I'm going to give you an opportunity to save some time and not read the rest of this chapter. Here's why: If you're like me and want to spend the majority of your time closing sales and working with brides-to-be, you don't have time to design a website.

You can spend your day making money and let someone else do the work by visiting www.EvansSalesSolutions.com. Ok, the shameless plug is over. Let's get on with it.

1. "I Don't Care – I Won't be Back" Rule

It's a hard reality that many people couldn't care less about your website—the same website that you spent thousands of dollars and hundreds of hours developing. Many people will visit and then leave your website without thinking twice about it.

While there's always the dream that your customers will form an emotional attachment to your business, reality is that, in most cases, an emotional attachment never develops. Therefore, it's important to remember what the purpose of your website is, and while I understand that it's very hard for some people not to form an emotional attachment to their own website, you need to always remember that your customers probably couldn't care less. Your web visitors want good information in an organized manner, delivered quickly, and they'll be happy. They're not going to go to bed and dreaming about your website no matter how much money you spent or how many hours it took to develop it.

One major point to remember is that your website is not your brochure. I understand this sets a normal thinking on its head, but it's true. Think of it this way: if you visit a website once and receive most of the information you need, then you go back and visit that page a second time a week later and the information is the same, what are the chances you'll return to that website a third time?

Statistically, we know that there's no chance of someone returning to your website more than twice if the information doesn't change. It's important to update your website and, at a bare minimum, rearrange the information so that the site always looks new and fresh. One of the biggest mistakes made, particularly by smaller mom-and-pop businesses, is posting the information on the web and then leaving it. It's important to provide accurate and timely information, but it's equally important to provide a wide range of information that changes regularly.

2. Four-Second Rule

No, this isn't the four- or five-second rule that we've all come to know when we were kids and dropped something on the ground just as we went to place it in our mouth. This is the four second rule that applies to your website as your prospects or customers are about to make a decision on how long they're going to spend looking at your information.

You should be able to look at the home page of any site and figure out what the site is about within four seconds. If you can't, the site is a failure. People simply don't have enough time to try to ascertain what it is you're trying to do with your website.

I find it amazing how many wedding professionals miss the mark and don't understand that their website should be designed to do exactly what direct mail does—that being, to motivate people to contact you for more information. I've seen hundreds of wedding professionals put so much information on their website that it's impossible to tell exactly what they do. The result is their page is cluttered and presents so many different concepts that any bride-to-be would be confused.

Then, that same wedding professional spends several hundred dollars to have their website optimized so that they can get to the top of the search engines. While it's true that if you're at the top of the search engines, you will have more visitors; it doesn't mean you will have more sales. A poorly designed page will be viewed; it just won't make you money. Take an honest look at your website and decide if in four seconds or less you can tell what you do.

3. "I Designed It Myself" Rule

It seems many wedding professionals, because they are smaller mom-and-pop operations, have a tendency to design their websites themselves. As we discussed in the direct-mail chapter of this book, just because you have the ability to buy programs that will allow you to design web pages, it doesn't mean you should do it. There's a reason why people go to school to learn web design.

A bride-to-be can buy a camera and have her friend shoot pictures at her wedding, but the results will be different than if she had hired a professional photographer. Professional photographers hate the idea that someone has such little respect for what they do that they would consider an amateur's work to be as good as their own. However, many professional photographers still feel perfectly comfortable selecting their best images and making a website, expecting that their business will be enhanced.

I understand that many web design organizations are little more than people who purchased a computer and present themselves as professionals, but that's not to say that there are professionals available, who have for years studied how to create the best possible web page. It's your job to find someone who is professional and allow him or her to enhance your business by creating a professional website.

4. "What the Heck Is That?" Rule

The "What the Heck Is That?" Rule is simple. If a bride-to-be comes to your website and sees anything on your page that makes her say, "What the heck is that?"—you lose.

For some reason, many wedding professionals believe that cursors with fancy tails or humorous pictures of their pets are things that the bride might be interested in seeing. Nothing could be further from the truth, and this type of distraction on your website will only serve to limit your website success. Here are some of the things to avoid on your website:

- Dancing cursor tails of <u>any kind</u>
- Family pictures
- Pet pictures
- Silly playful buttons
- Cartoon images
- Wedding bloopers
- Dishonest claims
- Unbelievable claims
- Phony offers
- Back button blocking
- Accepting payments on an unsecured page
- Phishing for information
- Pop-ups

5. The "I'm Lost and Can't Get Out" Rule

I'm amazed at what seems like such a simple idea seems to be misunderstood by so many wedding professionals. Many times, as

I'm surfing the web, I come to website that will provide me an opportunity to navigate deeper into the page, yet will not provide me with an opportunity to navigate away from the page. There seems to be some belief that by forcing me to stay on their web page for a longer period of time, I'm going to become more inclined to purchase product. Obviously, the longer I'm forced to be a page when I want to go to another page, the more frustrated I become. In my particular case, I become much less likely to order products or, for that matter ever, visit their website again.

For me, nothing is as frustrating as getting the information you need or the information you want, and then not being able to use the back button to leave the page. Each time I click on the back button and find I can't leave that web page the more determined I become to never do business with that wedding professional.

My experience has been that there are different niches within the wedding industry that seem more inclined to use this type of deceptive practice. For some reason, it seems to me that websites of disc jockeys and videographers seem to employ this type of practice more than most other wedding professionals. It may have something to do with the average age of the person who runs those businesses. I'm hesitant to make an indictment with too broad a brush, because obviously, this doesn't apply to everyone. However, it's common enough that I've identified a trend based on business type.

Think of it this way: Someone visits your home. You have a great visit. They spend a couple hours with you, and you become friends. You then have an opportunity to convey information to them that you wanted them to have. Then, when they decide to leave, they discover that you have locked the front door and they cannot get out. How long do you believe that they would be your friends?

I'm amazed that there are actually people in the world who believe by locking me into their web page, I will do business with them. It simply doesn't work; it's bad business and should not be done.

6. Navigational Failure Rule

The navigational structure of your website is the backbone to providing the information your client or prospective client may need. If you don't have a clearly defined navigational structure, people are going to get lost. In the world we live in today, people will not invest the time it may take to figure out what you had in mind when you designed the page. They're not going to fight with a messy navigational structure; they're simply going to go to another page.

One of the most common mistakes made regarding navigation on a website is having different types of navigation structures and buttons within the same site and having poorly worded links that so the visitor doesn't know where he or she should go. My favorite saying to my staff when we're developing a web page is that we need to "do it with crayons", meaning it has to be so simple that virtually anybody can understand where it goes.

Your kids may love to play Marco Polo and spend hours each day splashing around a pool with their eyes closed, but I'll bet the average bride-to-be doesn't want to take a course in stellar navigation to find her way through your website.

Another common problem that doesn't get much attention is the order in which your buttons appear. Many times, particularly with organizations where the people who visit the website are familiar with what that organization does, there is a tendency to build the link structure based on needs and not on any common structure you find across many different sites. For example, in the middle of many pages, you run across a picture, or certain parts of the picture, that are, in fact, links to other pages. You move your mouse across the image, and as you move from the head to the torso to the feet, different links pop-up so that you can go to different pages. While this is fairly cool, it's very confusing to people who haven't visited your website before.

It's much more efficient and provides an easier user interface if you create a link and buttons structure that remain consistent throughout your site. The more trouble it is for someone to navigate to your site, the more chances you will have that they will never visit your site again.

7. The Too Much Rule

Yes, it's called a web page, and a web page can have quite a bit of information. However, that doesn't mean you have to cram all your material on one page. It's very easy to keep adding material to your home page until it gets out of control.

With so much content vying for attention, it's difficult for the eyes to find the focal point. People get confused, and they leave. A long web page means you have failed to organize your site properly. It probably represents a combination of not planning your site and poor navigation.

8. The Abracadabra Rule

Don't confuse web design with a magic trick. In a magic trick, you show the audience your right hand and perform the trick with your left. In web design, you tell them where you're going first—and then go there. People have expectations about websites, and they don't like surprises. It will certainly confuse them, and it could make them want to leave and find a site that's less confusing.

If you're a wedding photographer, your visitors expect your website to look like it belongs to a wedding photographer—not to someone who is going to the thrift sale.

Speaking of magic tricks, links should be clearly labeled so your visitors won't be surprised when they click.

If you use a vague link description or just say "Click Here" and don't tell people where they'll end up, they could be horribly surprised when they click the link

9. The Flash It Rule

Just as a raincoat is a tool that can be used for good or evil purposes, Adobe Flash is also just a tool that can be used for good or evil. It all comes down to how it's used and who is using it.

Unfortunately, there's a tendency to misuse Flash, and because of space, I can't go into every detail. Nevertheless, just because you took time to learn Flash doesn't mean every bride is going to sit through a 15-minute introduction to your website every time she visits. If she has to watch a boring, soundless, twenty-second flash intro with no option to skip it, she's gone.

Forgetting to put a "Skip Intro" button, forcing visitors to see your stupid Flash Splash page every time they visit, is a big mistake. The problem could be "solved" by setting a cookie so that visitors only see the animation once unless they click a button to "play it again."

Putting a "Skip Intro" button on the page, we all realize, can signify that the content on the page is worthless. Good web designers only put content that must be viewed on a page. By giving them the option to skip this material, you're saying it's not worth seeing. If it isn't worth seeing, why do you have it on your site in the first place?

If you must have a "Skip Intro" button, make it big enough so people can see it and have it available as soon as the animation starts. Don't wait 10 seconds to load the button.

In regards to making people listen to music, if you have (original) music in your Flash animation, give people the option to turn off the music.

On the up side, when Flash works, the results are powerful.

10. If I Build It, They Will Come

Simply having a page on the web isn't enough to attract visitors. You need to continually promote your page on all literature and advertising that you participate in. If you do not promote the page everywhere, nobody will know about it.

When you post your page, you should start funneling all activity through the page. When a bride needs information, don't mail it; put the information online. When she wants to see samples, put them on your page. The best way to increase the activity on your page is to first make sure the information is valuable, usable, and on point. Then make your website the center of your promotional universe.

Quick Start Guide

One of the challenges software companies face when selling product to new customers is that people tend to purchase software, rip into the box, ignoring three or four stickers that will say "READ THIS FIRST", and start installing their software.

When the consumer runs into a problem, they have a tendency to jump on the phone and start screaming at technicians when the truth is that it's their own fault. They didn't read the instructions.

Recently, many software companies have started including a Quick Start Guide. A sheet that gives the bare minimum amount of information so the purchaser, whom we know probably won't read the directions can see two or three mandatory steps to use the software. It reduces the client's frustration and reduces angry calls to the software technicians.

This is my Quick Start Guide. You may use it, but understand you won't know the intricacies of the program. There will be features you don't use because you didn't take time to read the manual, but I understand you're busy. Use the Quick Start Guide, understanding the following:

- You will do things and not know why. Others will tell you it's not right, and you won't know why they are wrong.
- The system I outline ALWAYS works if you work the system.
- We do offer technical support through our coaching program.

Quick Start 1 – Do the following:

1. Make every staff member a salesperson.

2. Change your verbiage. Eliminate contracts and deposits and replace with agreements and initial investments.

3. Understand who your customer is. Draw a profile.

4. Understand that brides buy what they want, not what they need.

5. Cancel all advertising except bridal shows.

6. Only book face-to-face visits at shows, nothing else.

7. Conduct a full presentation to every bride face-to-face.

8. Tell her about 10-20 features of your product.

9. Ask her to buy.

10. Go back to number one.

Quick Start 2 – DO NOT do the following:

1. Listen to people who haven't read the book.

2. Listen to people who have read the book tell you it won't work.

3. Change a word of the scripts provided.

4. Advertise in anything except bridal shows and direct mail until you reach your goal.

That's the Quick Start Guide. You really should read the book, but this should get you started.

Certified Wedding Pros

WEDDING MERCHANTS BUSINESS ACADEMY

Over 40 Years Experience

Will & Patti Hegarty produce the Bridal Fashion Debut, America's biggest bridal show. This year they are producing the sixth annual Wedding MBA convention, America's largest educational event dedicated to the business side of the wedding business.

Will began as a wedding photographer at the age of 15. He has a degree in business from Arizona State University and is the founding president of Rockford Fosgate car audio, which went public in 2001. Patti has her Masters in Education. Will and his employees have documented over 5,000 weddings over the last 40 years.

Will & Patti met at a wedding, where he was the photographer and she was a bridesmaid. They organized their first bridal show in June 1992 with 28 exhibitors. In 2009, their shows each had over 1100 exhibitors, the largest in America.

Learn from their successes and challenges distilled from 40 years in the wedding business, plus other expert speakers in each wedding specialty.

For Details Visit

www.WeddingMBA.com

There have been times when I needed help, but I didn't know where to turn." – D. Barnett

Chris Evans Business Coaching

- Show You How to Achieve Greater Returns with Less Work
- Help You Create Greater Profit
- Develop Your Team
- Lower Your Costs
- Rediscover Your Passion
- Navigate Through This Challenging Economy
- Help Create Accountability
- Provide Access to a Wedding Business Expert

Chris Evans Business Coaching will help with any needs that your business may have. We have access to thousands of services.

The size of your business doesn't matter. We have worked with individual wedding professionals as well as major Fortune 500 companies. We can help!

"Soon after I started producing bridal shows, it became painfully aware to me that many of the wedding professionals I knew were great at what they did, but they just weren't that great at business. Many who were good at business just needed some help. That's when we created Chris Evans International."

– Chris Evans . . . .